10

Mexico

Julia Garbus, *Book Editor*

GREENHAVEN PRESS
A part of Gale, Cengage Learning

GALE
CENGAGE Learning·

Farmington Hills, Mich • San Francisco • New York • Waterville, Maine
Meriden, Conn • Mason, Ohio • Chicago

Patricia Coryell, *Vice President & Publisher, New Products & GVRL*
Douglas Dentino, *Manager, New Products*
Judy Galens, *Acquisitions Editor*

Articles in Greenhaven Press anthologies are often edited for length to meet page require-ments. In addition, original titles of these works are changed to clearly present the main thesis and to explicitly indicate the author's opinion. Every effort is made to ensure that Greenhaven Press accurately reflects the original intent of the authors. Every effort has been made to trace the owners of copyrighted material.

Cover image © Jess Kraft/Shutterstock.com.

LIBRARY OF CONGRESS CATALOGING-IN-PUBLICATION DATA

Mexico / Julia Garbus, book editor.
    pages cm. -- (Introducing issues with opposing viewpoints)
    Includes bibliographical references and index.
    Audience: Grade 9 to 12.
    ISBN 978-0-7377-7237-1 (hardcover)
    1. Mexico--Economic conditions--1994---Juvenile literature. 2. Mexico--Social conditions --1970---Juvenile literature. I. Garbus, Julia.
    HC135.M545116 2015
    330.972--dc23

                                                                        2014022956

Printed in the United States of America
1 2 3 4 5 6 7 18 17 16 15 14

Contents

Chapter 3: How Should Mexico Approach the Drug War?

Foreword

Indulging in a wide spectrum of ideas, beliefs, and perspectives is a critical cornerstone of democracy. After all, it is often debates over differences of opinion, such as whether to legalize abortion, how to treat prisoners, or when to enact the death penalty, that shape our society and drive it forward. Such diversity of thought is frequently regarded as the hallmark of a healthy and civilized culture. As the Reverend Clifford Schutjer of the First Congregational Church in Mansfield, Ohio, declared in a 2001 sermon, "Surrounding oneself with only like-minded people, restricting what we listen to or read only to what we find agreeable is irresponsible. Refusing to entertain doubts once we make up our minds is a subtle but deadly form of arrogance." With this advice in mind, Introducing Issues with Opposing Viewpoints books aim to open readers' minds to the critically divergent views that comprise our world's most important debates.

Introducing Issues with Opposing Viewpoints simplifies for students the enormous and often overwhelming mass of material now available via print and electronic media. Collected in every volume is an array of opinions that captures the essence of a particular controversy or topic. Introducing Issues with Opposing Viewpoints books embody the spirit of nineteenth-century journalist Charles A. Dana's axiom: "Fight for your opinions, but do not believe that they contain the whole truth, or the only truth." Absorbing such contrasting opinions teaches students to analyze the strength of an argument and compare it to its opposition. From this process readers can inform and strengthen their own opinions, or be exposed to new information that will change their minds. Introducing Issues with Opposing Viewpoints is a mosaic of different voices. The authors are statesmen, pundits, academics, journalists, corporations, and ordinary people who have felt compelled to share their experiences and ideas in a public forum. Their words have been collected from newspapers, journals, books, speeches, interviews, and the Internet, the fastest growing body of opinionated material in the world.

Introducing Issues with Opposing Viewpoints shares many of the well-known features of its critically acclaimed parent series, Opposing Viewpoints. The articles are presented in a pro/con format, allowing readers to absorb divergent perspectives side by side. Active reading questions preface each viewpoint, requiring the student to approach the material thoughtfully and carefully. Useful charts, graphs, and cartoons supplement each article. A thorough introduction provides readers with crucial background on an issue. An annotated bibliography points the reader toward articles, books, and websites that contain additional information on the topic. An appendix of organizations to contact contains a wide variety of charities, nonprofit organizations, political groups, and private enterprises that each hold a position on the issue at hand. Finally, a comprehensive index allows readers to locate content quickly and efficiently.

Introducing Issues with Opposing Viewpoints is also significantly different from Opposing Viewpoints. As the series title implies, its presentation will help introduce students to the concept of opposing viewpoints and learn to use this material to aid in critical writing and debate. The series' four-color, accessible format makes the books attractive and inviting to readers of all levels. In addition, each viewpoint has been carefully edited to maximize a reader's understanding of the content. Short but thorough viewpoints capture the essence of an argument. A substantial, thought-provoking essay question placed at the end of each viewpoint asks the student to further investigate the issues raised in the viewpoint, compare and contrast two authors' arguments, or consider how one might go about forming an opinion on the topic at hand. Each viewpoint contains sidebars that include at-a-glance information and handy statistics. A Facts About section located in the back of the book further supplies students with relevant facts and figures.

Following in the tradition of the Opposing Viewpoints series, Greenhaven Press continues to provide readers with invaluable exposure to the controversial issues that shape our world. As John Stuart Mill once wrote: "The only way in which a human being can make some approach to knowing the whole of a subject is by hearing what can be said about it by persons of every variety of opinion and studying all modes in which it can be looked at by every character of mind. No wise man ever acquired his wisdom in any mode but this." It is to this principle that Introducing Issues with Opposing Viewpoints books are dedicated.

Introduction

"Mexico has the potential to become a world-class economic and political powerhouse. But it's not there yet. Several necessary ingredients are missing."

—Edgardo Buscaglia, president of the Instituto de Acción Ciudadana in Mexico, May 30, 2013

Delicious tacos. Beautiful beaches. Drug war deaths. A flood of illegal immigrants. Many Americans have a black-or-white view of their neighbor to the south. Is it a vacation paradise or a violent, bloodstained land its citizens long to leave? The answer is both—and neither. Mexico is complicated. In many ways, it is a country in between. Geographically, Mexico is sandwiched between the world's only superpower, the United States, and the small, even less developed Central American countries of Guatemala and Belize. Economically and politically, it is developing. In terms of how its people live, Mexico is in between, too: as a 2012 Wilson Center report puts it, the nation is "poor no more, developed not yet."[1]

Mexico is big. It's the fourteenth-largest country in the world, about three times the size of Texas. Its population tops 123 million; Mexico City, with more than 20 million people, is the third-largest metropolitan area in the world. The country consists of thirty-one states plus the capital, Mexico City, which is its own district. Its landscape is varied, including tropical zones, beautiful beaches, high mountains, gigantic canyons, and sprawling deserts; so many species of animals live in Mexico that it is considered "megadiverse."[2]

Beginning in about 1500 B.C., major indigenous civilizations populated Mexico: the Olmec, Maya, Teotihuacán, Toltec, and finally the Aztec, a highly developed civilization whose huge empire contained up to 11 million people. Spanish explorer Hernán Cortés arrived in 1519, bent on conquest. He defeated the Aztec, destroyed their capital, and claimed the territory for Spain. Smallpox, which arrived along with the Europeans, decimated the indigenous population. Over the next three hundred years, Spain treated Mexico's mixed race (*mestizo*) and native peoples badly and drained the New World country's resources to benefit itself.

In 1810 Mexicans began fighting for independence, and by 1821 the Spanish had withdrawn. During the rest of the nineteenth century, Mexico struggled to defend itself from more-powerful countries that tried to take advantage of the new republic. In the 1830s, American settlers in Texas fought successfully for independence from Mexico, a struggle that included the famous stand at the Alamo. The United States invaded Mexico in 1846 and forced it to sell its northern territories to the United States, including present-day California, Arizona, Nevada, Utah, and parts of Colorado and Wyoming. France took over governing Mexico in the 1860s, leaving only after the United States demanded it.

Soon after the French left, Mexican politician Porfirio Díaz began a lockdown spanning nearly three decades that featured economic modernization and political suppression. Finally Mexicans overthrew their homegrown dictator, led by revolutionaries such as Pancho Villa and Emiliano Zapata. Although the next decade was politically turbulent, it produced the Mexican constitution of 1917, still in effect, which set out social rights, limited the power of the Catholic Church, and redistributed land from the rich to the peasants and small farmers. The country stabilized in 1929, and a new political party was created, eventually named the Partido Revolucionario Institucional, or Institutional Revolutionary Party (PRI). In the 1930s, President Lázaro Cárdenas made important land reforms, promoted education, and nationalized Mexico's railroads and booming oil industry.

The PRI remained in power for seventy-one years. Although Mexicans voted, corruption and fraud made election results meaningless. The country continued to grow economically throughout the twentieth century, but most of its people remained poor. Mexico entered into the North American Free Trade Agreement (NAFTA) in 1993. This agreement eliminated tariffs (taxes on imports and exports) between Canada, the United States, and Mexico. The PRI's grip on the presidency ended in 2000, when Mexicans elected a president from the Partido Acción Nacional, or National Action Party (PAN). Several different parties share power now, and the current president, Enrique Peña Nieto, is a member of the PRI.

For many years, illegal drugs flowed from South America through Mexico to the United States. After the Colombian government dismantled that country's cocaine cartels in the late 1980s, Mexican drug lords began distributing the drug as well as transporting it, battling each other for turf. President Felipe Calderón, elected in 2006, mobilized government troops to fight the cartels. Although the military forces eliminated many drug kingpins, without their leaders the cartels splintered, creating new, even more violent groups. More than sixty thousand people died in drug-related violence from 2006 to 2012.

Today Mexico has many points of pride. Elections are free. The country is Latin America's largest importer and exporter—sixteenth in the volume of global trade. President Peña Nieto, who took office in 2012, has begun to reform education, labor markets, financial regulations, fiscal affairs, elections rules, and the energy sector. Mexican immigration to the United States is at a virtual standstill, showing that its citizens are willing to stay in the country; many immigrants have even returned.

Still, it would be inaccurate to say that Mexico is thriving. Almost half the population is poor. Out of the thirty-four member countries of the Organization for Economic Co-operation and Development, Mexico has the lowest household income and the second-highest level of income inequality. Political corruption is a major problem. About 90 percent of Mexicans surveyed by the organization Transparency International called the country's political parties and police corrupt; more than 80 percent thought the court system, legislature, and public servants were corrupt. More than half of those who had had contact with the police or the court system had bribed an official.

How can Mexico build a better future? *Introducing Issues with Opposing Viewpoints: Mexico* explores this question. The authors in this collection debate Mexico's overall outlook, President Peña Nieto's reforms, corruption and human rights abuses, immigration, and the fight against drug cartels and violence. The viewpoints help readers form their own conclusions about Mexico's challenges and opportunities in the twenty-first century.

Notes

1. Luis de la Calle and Luis Rubio, *Mexico: A Middle Class Society; Poor No More, Developed Not Yet*, Woodrow Wilson International Center for Scholars, January 2012. www.wilsoncenter.org/sites

/default/files/Mexico%20A%20Middle%20Class%20Society.pdf.

2. World Bank, "Biodiversity: National System of Protected Natural Areas (SINAP), Mexico," 2011. http://web.worldbank.org/WBSITE/EXTERNAL/TOPICS/ENVIRONMENT/EXTBIODIVERSITY/0,,contentMDK:23264975~pagePK:148956~piPK:216618~theSitePK:400953,00.html.

Chapter 1

What Does the Future Hold for Mexico?

A Mexican citizen votes in the presidential election of 2012. A sign in the background reads "Your vote is free and secret."

Enrique Peña Nieto Elected President of Mexico

> *"Peña Nieto's victory sets the course for a new direction for the future of Mexico."*

PR Newswire

The following viewpoint, a news release on PR Newswire from 2012, outlines the goals of newly elected president Enrique Peña Nieto for the future of Mexico. The viewpoint states that Peña Nieto plans to fight organized crime, reduce poverty levels, and improve the educational system. Tackling these key issues, Peña Nieto contends, will improve the well-being of society and broaden Mexico's international relations. PR Newswire is a news and information distribution service for the public relations and communications industries.

AS YOU READ, CONSIDER THE FOLLOWING QUESTIONS:

1. How many national and regional commitments did Peña Nieto promise while campaigning for the presidency, according to the author?
2. What is the social purpose of a renewed free-market economy according to Peña Nieto, as quoted by PR Newswire?
3. What does the election of Peña Nieto by a significant margin represent, according to the author?

Marking an important generational shift in Mexican leadership, 49 million Mexicans voted Sunday to elect Enrique Peña Nieto as the 89th President of Mexico. According to Mexico's Federal Electoral Institute Peña Nieto, the 45-year-old former Governor of the State of Mexico, will garner about 38 percent of the votes cast, approximately seven percent higher than the second place finisher. He will take office December 1, 2012.

Peña Nieto's victory sets the course for a new direction for the future of Mexico. The president-elect built his campaign on an aggressive and highly detailed set of 255 national and regional "commitments" on which he has pledged to deliver. It is this style of public accountability and transparency that has positioned him as a staunch departure from the past reputation of his party, the Institutional Revolutionary Party (commonly known as the PRI).

In his victory speech, President-elect Peña Nieto stressed the importance of ending the political polarization in Mexico that has prevented the adoption of critical reforms; continuing the fight against drug trafficking and violence; and promoting economic growth policies that help alleviate poverty in the country. Below are translated excerpts from his victory speech, delivered early Monday morning:

> I will lead a democratic presidency that understands the changes the country has experienced over the last decades, and acts according to the new democratic realities that we enjoy today. A full democracy bursting with personal liberties and social participation. I will lead a modern and responsible presidency, open to criticisms, always ready to listen and one that will take all Mexicans into account.

> . . . I reiterate what I have already said in this very hall during the campaign; whoever does not show a firm commitment to

Mexican president Enrique Peña Nieto (center) signs into law a 2014 energy reform bill, one of several key initiatives that he believes will strengthen Mexico's future.

democracy, personal liberties and transparency, has no place in this project to transform Mexico. We are a new generation. We will not return to the past. My government will have its eyes set on the future. Mexico has already changed.

We will build the results-driven democracy that Mexicans deserve, starting with an effective, honest, transparent and accountable government. A government that fights corruption head-on. A democratic government is a government that strictly observes and ensures the rule of law.

The fight against crime will continue. Yes, with a new strategy to reduce violence and protect, above all, the lives of Mexicans. In the face of organized crime, there will be neither negotiation nor truce.

We need to promote a renewed free-market economy, but one with a social purpose. An economy that creates more jobs and better distributes wealth, to combat the poverty and inequality that still today affect millions of Mexican families.

Peña Nieto has been particularly outspoken about his priorities for economic growth, job creation and poverty alleviation across Mexico.

Crime and Drug-Related Violence Are the Top Concerns in Mexico

Percentage of Mexicans saying the following are very big problems:

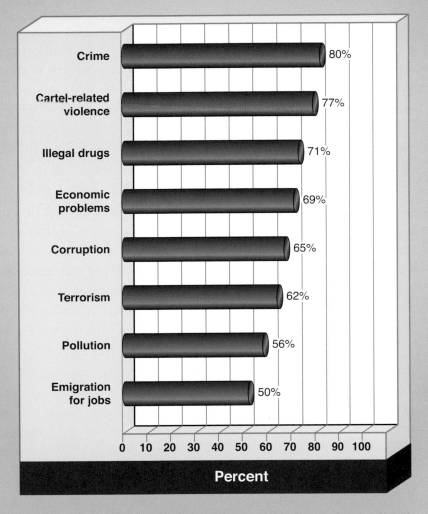

Taken from: Pew Research Center Global Attitudes Project, "Crime and Drug Cartels Top Concerns in Mexico," August 31, 2011, p. 6.

He has promised to return much needed attention to social issues gone largely unaddressed in recent years, including a commitment to dramatically increasing high school completion rates and generating more than a million jobs a year through greater economic competition and investments in infrastructure.

In addition, he has pledged to continue the fight against organized crime and drug trafficking that have riddled Mexico in recent years. To ensure his success, Peña Nieto has tapped recently retired Colombian Police Chief, General Oscar Naranjo, to serve as an advisor on an assertive array of crime-fighting measures. General Naranjo, decorated as one of the "world's leading crime fighters" by law enforcement agencies around the globe, will be a valuable resource in advising how to strengthen our enforcement and improve cooperation with other countries.

Moreover, Peña Nieto has vowed to regain Mexico's foreign policy leadership in Latin American and to continue to foster strong ties with its North American neighbors, the United States and Canada. This includes growing NAFTA beyond a trade zone and integrating economies through greater investments in manufacturing and finance. He has also affirmed his intention to pursue more economic opportunities and integration with Asia and the European Union so as to diversity Mexico's economy.

Peña Nieto's election by such a significant margin represents a generational shift and clear departure from the old notions of the PRI. He has surrounded himself with a cadre of young technocrats who have brought a wealth of innovative ideas, a forward-looking vision, and a new direction. Even prominent political leaders like former President Vicente Fox—a member of an opposing party—have advocated that the country support Peña Nieto.

EVALUATING THE AUTHOR'S ARGUMENTS

In this viewpoint, PR Newswire and President Enrique Peña Nieto sound an optimistic note about the future of Mexico and the country's potential for social improvement and economic development. How is this view different from that of Larry Kaplow, the author of the following viewpoint? Explain your answer citing from each viewpoint.

Mexico's False Dawn

Larry Kaplow

In the following viewpoint, Larry Kaplow questions whether recent improvements in Mexican society reflect long-term growth. While crime levels have dropped, he contends that the government has not yet implemented the institutional changes needed to sustain this trend. In addition, while the nation's economy is improving, he wonders whether this is a sign of future prosperity. Long-term growth will require Mexico to improve its educational system and infrastructure, Kaplow argues. While the future of the nation shows promise, the author believes it is too soon to declare this Mexico's "new dawn." Kaplow is a writer living in Mexico City, who has written for the Associated Press and for publications such as *Atlantic Monthly* and *Newsweek*.

"Is this country really changing for the better, or is it just on a lucky roll?"

AS YOU READ, CONSIDER THE FOLLOWING QUESTIONS:

1. According to the author, *Reforma* counted how many gang-related murders in Mexico in 2012?
2. How is cocaine use in the United States related to the crime rate in Mexico, according to Kaplow?
3. A study cited by the author claims that middle-class incomes start at how much per day?

exico begins the new year with unusual optimism. People here have new hope that the worst of the drug war has passed, and the economy has returned to growth after a brutal recession. But in Mexico, things often aren't what they seem: Is this country really changing for the better, or is it just on a lucky roll?

The country's promise—and its problems—have been on full display during President Enrique Peña Nieto's first few weeks in office. Residents of the notoriously violent city of Juárez enjoyed the first weekend without a homicide in five years—but the majority of the police force of another town in central Mexico resigned amid a spate of attacks. Families flocked to downtown Mexico City over Christmas to skate around the ice rink that is set up every year—but just three weeks ago, the same area had been the scene of mayhem and violence

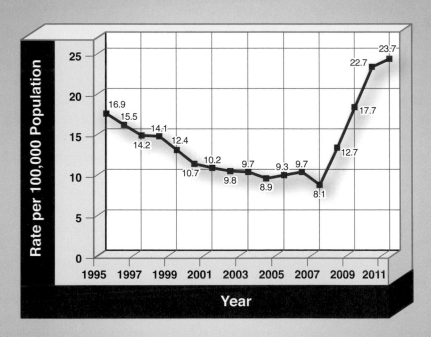

Homicide Rate in Mexico, 1995–2011

Note: Rate for intentional homicide.

Taken from: Cory Molzahn, Octavio Rodriguez Ferreira, and David A. Shirk, "Drug Violence in Mexico: Data and Analysis Through 2012," Trans-Border Institute, University of San Diego, February 2013, p. 5.

as protesters demonstrated against what they saw as Peña Nieto's fraudulent election victory.

Much of Mexico remains very violent, but the killings have ebbed somewhat from the worst days of the drug war. In recent years, its homicide rate has stood at more than three and a half times that of the United States. But there has been incremental improvement: In a (probably incomplete) tally, the daily *Reforma* counted about 9,800 gang-related murders in 2012—down from 12,366 in 2011. Alejandro Hope, director of security policy at the Mexican Competitiveness Institute, says all murder—perhaps a better indicator than just cartel-related counts—was down about 8 percent in 2012.

So though there were still four times as many gang murders as in 2007, last year's drop has brought a sense of relief. In Juárez, businesses are reopening and night life is returning. Vacationers flocked back to Acapulco after a massive military effort there. It reminds me of the more extreme situation I saw covering the Iraq war, as people became almost giddy in 2007 when bombings dropped from several times a week to just a few times a month. There, people used to say that a dying man is happy to find out he's only sick. U.S. commanders called it a "tolerable" level of violence.

But preventing another deadly spiral of violence depends on how much the change is due to strengthened Mexican institutions. In a recent conversation, Hope listed encouraging signs: The government doubled and tripled security budgets over recent years, and the police and military improved their tactics. The security forces have been going after midlevel narcos, which cut cartel capabilities but don't create the violent power vacuums that occur when kingpins are toppled. Others note that the feds have smartly disbanded entire local police forces, which are often too corrupt or intimidated to do any good, before starting anti-crime sweeps.

But the drop in violence could also be fueled by less encouraging factors. When it comes to Juárez, for instance, nobody can agree on the reasons behind the dramatic drop in violence. Mexico may be less deadly because cartels have sorted out their turf and consequently have less reason to fight. A drop in cocaine use in the United States, Hope said, has probably reduced shipments to the north, resulting in fewer drug-related killings. And one crime expert wrote that the cartel wars may have expended the supply of street-level killers—for now.

"It could always start up again," Hope says. "We're going to be battling organized crime for generations."

Last year raised doubts that law enforcement is up for that battle. In June, three federal police were killed by their colleagues in a food court at Mexico City's airport, apparently as one group tried to arrest the others for smuggling. Another 14 *federales* were charged with ambushing a car carrying CIA employees and a Mexican Navy captain in August. The federal police has been an independent force and was key to former President Felipe Calderón's anti-drug strategy—but Peña Nieto is now folding it into another ministry and forming a "gendarmerie" to fight cartels. And though the Marines scored big when they killed the country's most feared cartel leader, Zetas chief Heriberto Lazcano, in a gunfight, they actually didn't know who he was at the time and his corpse was quickly stolen.

Similar questions surround Mexico's economy. It has approached or surpassed 4 percent growth each of the past three years, but whether it can continue its progress remains anyone's guess. Some think it can: A recent rosy-with-caveats report in the *Economist* stated that the country's turnaround will probably make it one of the world's top 10 economies in 2020, while the World Bank reported that, between 2000 and 2010, 17 percent of the population joined Mexico's middle class.

Read between the lines, however, and Mexico's economic success story becomes more complicated. The World Bank study about a booming middle class, for instance, defined middle-class incomes as starting at only $10 a day per person. A recent U.N. survey of 18 Latin American countries showed nearly all of them reducing poverty over the last decade—with all but two doing so faster than Mexico. And the new middle class often still relies on remittances, which total more than $21 billion annually, from relatives in the United States. Those funds still surpass the country's foreign tourism revenue—it's the age-old "exportation" of Mexico's unemployment for cash.

Teachers in Mexico City march in protest against the educational reforms proposed by President Enrique Peña Nieto in 2013. Aiming to repair Mexico's historically weak school systems, the reforms require teachers to undergo mandatory performance appraisals.

Mexico's economic progress is also still tied to forces beyond its control. The new economy has been aided by the end of the U.S. recession, which has improved exports and released pent-up demand. Chinese wages are rising, making Mexican factories more competitive. Decent oil prices have also been key, as energy revenues fund a third of the country's budget.

But leaving itself at the whim of outside forces isn't a recipe for continued success. Long-term free market prosperity requires better education, infrastructure, and equal opportunity enforced by law. The country has made progress, holding three messy but competitive elections since 2000 under a more powerful elections commission. The Supreme Court is more independent and has issued important rulings, such as reining in some military powers. There's been a bloom of civil society groups using freedom-of-information laws to extract data from the government, evaluating schools, recording human rights abuses, and exposing corruption. And Peña Nieto is pushing a plan to improve the notoriously poor schools by vetting the country's teachers, who are now nearly impossible to fire.

Peña Nieto described the problem at his inauguration, saying, "We are a nation that grows in two gears. There is a Mexico of progress and development, but there is another as well that exists in backwardness and poverty."

There are still plenty of elites who probably value their privileges more than the patriotic feeling they'd get from seeing their country advance. Mexico has had long periods of macroeconomic growth, including from 1940 to 1982, but it was often built on harsh conditions and little mobility for most Mexicans. Today, monopolies or duopolies still exist in fields ranging from food production to broadcast television, and billionaire Carlos Slim's conglomerate still controls the telephone and Internet markets. Well-connected criminals and informal syndicates extract protection money and determine who can mine coal, produce avocados, and even open street stands. Oil profits are reportedly sapped by corruption and smuggling within the state oil company, which Peña Nieto promises to reform. The self-styled "president for life" of the teachers union, political kingmaker Elba Esther Gordillo, has vowed to fight Peña Nieto's school reforms. Meanwhile, the country fell four years straight from 2008 through 2011 on Transparency International's Corruption Perceptions Index.

New regulations must simultaneously encourage growth while protecting workers from abusive corporate bosses. The business community hailed new labor laws issued in December that make it easier to hire and fire as a sign of a new Mexico. That sounds good for growth, but labor activists fear a blast from the past, saying the law preserves exploitative practices like coercing workers to sign repeated temporary contracts in order to avoid paying overtime and benefits. They say the reforms also still allow politically connected unions to enter factories without employee approval and get paid by bosses to silence workers. No wonder full-timers still live in poverty.

And when it comes to the business of government, political rules leave polls more beholden to parties than the public, with a one-term limit that makes mayors and governors rely on party machines for their next job. Additionally, the absence of a presidential runoff allowed Peña Nieto to win office with just 38 percent of the vote in a four-way race.

For now, Mexico and its new president have some momentum. But Mexicans know that good times can quickly turn bad. On New Year's Eve, revelers in Mexico City lit fireworks and street bonfires to ring in 2013—so many, in fact, that smog alerts had to be issued in the capital.

EVALUATING THE AUTHOR'S ARGUMENTS

In this viewpoint, Larry Kaplow is skeptical about whether recent improvements in Mexican society reflect long-term growth. Having read his arguments and the comments of the preceding viewpoint, what is your opinion on the matter? Explain your answer.

NAFTA Has Had a Positive Effect on Mexico

"Evidence points to Mexico . . . as by far the biggest winner [in the North American Free Trade Agreement]."

The Canadian Press

In the following viewpoint, the Canadian Press, a news agency headquartered in Toronto, contends that the North American Free Trade Agreement (NAFTA) has had a positive impact on Mexico. NAFTA is a treaty that took effect in 1994 and eliminated restrictions on commerce between Mexico, the United States, and Canada. On NAFTA's twentieth anniversary, the author contends that Mexico has benefited the most from the agreement. Two decades after NAFTA's enactment, the author argues, Mexico has expanded its global reach, improved its economy, and has a growing middle class.

AS YOU READ, CONSIDER THE FOLLOWING QUESTIONS:

1. According to the author, who made his name as an anti-NAFTA crusader?
2. The Canadian Press claims that Mexico's exports are how much more in 2014 than they were in 1994?
3. Which industry in Mexico has been a major beneficiary of NAFTA, according to the author?

R oss Perot [a 1992 US presidential candidate] may have had it right after all about who would win under NAFTA.

The North American Free Trade Agreement was an important step for all three members, but the evidence points to Mexico—at the time the weak sister in the group that included two G7 economies, the United States and Canada—as by far the biggest winner.

On the 20th anniversary of the pact [2013], Mexico—in 1994, an insular, economic basket case—has in two decades emerged as a forward-looking country with expanding global reach, a handful of world-class corporations and a ballooning middle class.

Examining NAFTA's Impact on Mexico

Perot, who twice ran for U.S. president in the 1990s and made his name as an anti-NAFTA crusader, generally saw that coming although he focused his barbs on what the U.S. would lose in what he termed "the giant sucking sound of jobs going south."

Perot's fear was that U.S. firms would flock to where labour costs were cheapest. To an extent that has happened, and it can be argued that Canada too lost critical manufacturing jobs to Mexico.

While there are some in Mexico who would dispute the characterization of their country as the big winner, the numbers make a strong case.

FAST FACT

According to *The Economist*, Mexico's trade with the United States increased by 506 percent between 1993 and 2012.

Mexico under NAFTA had a rough start, because of a coincidental pesos crash just as the deal was getting under way. But the country has grown into the one of the more robust emerging economies with exports of about $1 billion a day, more than 10 times what they were in 1994.

Mexico is now estimated to be the world's 13th-largest economy with total output similar to Canada's, although on a per capita basis it still lags.

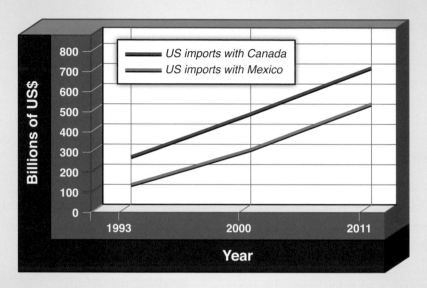

US Trade with Canada and Mexico Under NAFTA

Billions of US$

- US imports with Canada
- US imports with Mexico

800
700
600
500
400
300
200
100
0

1993   2000   2011

Year

Taken from: US Chamber of Commerce, "NAFTA Triumphant: Assessing Two Decades of Gains in Trade, Growth, and Jobs," November 2012, p. 5.

"I think NAFTA has been excellent for Mexico," says economist Jaime Serra Puche, the Mexican trade minister at the time, adding it would have worked even better if Mexico had not waited almost 20 years to bring in internal reforms to the economy.

"Now with the reforms that are finally taking place I think we are going to gain competitiveness and the platform that has been constructed mostly for exports and manufacturing is going to become stronger."

Manufacturing Catastrophe

Some of that has come at the expense of Canada, or so believes Jim Stanford, an economist with the Unifor union. Under the deal,

Mexico has gone from a bit player in the North American auto sector to the second-largest participant with almost 20 per cent of total production, compared with Canada's 16 per cent.

"Heavy truck shipments in Canada collapsed by 75 per cent between 2006 and 2011. It's an incredible example of a manufacturing catastrophe and NAFTA was absolutely a key part of it," he says.

Serra and others who have studied post-NAFTA impacts agree that Mexico's manufacturing sector, and particularly the auto industry, has been a big beneficiary.

But they don't give all the credit to the deal.

Even before 1994, Mexico had started on the road to trade liberalization and economic stability, by giving its central bank independence, for instance. NAFTA may have been the last and most important piece of the puzzle, but not the only one, they say.

Overall, trade deals are often oversold by both proponents and critics, says Angeles Villarreal, a trade specialist with the U.S. Congressional Research Service who co-authored a paper on the deal earlier this year.

"It didn't benefit as much as the optimists predicted, but also the negative effects weren't as severe. There weren't huge job losses," she says.

Mexico Is Transforming

On the plus side for Mexico, the auto industry has taken off, skills have improved and manufacturing has increased—and not just low-skilled factory jobs, she says.

On the negative side, there were losers as well, particularly firms propped up by high tariff walls and small subsistence farmers, although even here the evidence is unclear. Villarreal says it's difficult to separate the NAFTA effect on farming from that of land reform that came at about the same time.

Christopher Wilson of the Mexico Institute at the Woodrow Wilson International Center in Washington [D.C.] says while there were losers, NAFTA has to be considered an overall success for the country.

"Mexico at the time was the smallest, now the Mexican and Canadian economies are similar in size," he points out.

The North American Free Trade Agreement (NAFTA) benefited Mexico's manufacturing sector, especially the auto industry, which enjoyed an increase in skilled and factory jobs.

"One of the big stories in Mexico has been the slow but steady emergence of a middle class that's now about half of the country.

"It's not the same as the middle class as the U.S. or Canada, but it does mean they are not in poverty, they now own a car, they go to the movies, they take a vacation. It's transforming the country," he says.

EVALUATING THE AUTHOR'S ARGUMENTS

In this viewpoint, the Canadian Press maintains that Mexico was NAFTA's biggest winner. On the basis of what you have read, do you agree that NAFTA has had a positive effect on Mexico? Why or why not?

NAFTA Has Not Had a Positive Effect on Mexico

"[NAFTA's] end result [in Mexico] has been decades of economic failure by almost any economic or social indicator."

Mark Weisbrot, Stephan Lefebvre, and Joseph Sammut

In the following viewpoint, Mark Weisbrot, Stephan Lefebvre, and Joseph Sammut argue that the North American Free Trade Agreement (NAFTA) did not help Mexico's economy. NAFTA is a treaty that took effect in 1994, eliminating restrictions on commerce between Mexico, the United States, and Canada. The authors assert that NAFTA caused decades of economic failure in Mexico. If the trade agreement had been successful, the authors maintain, Mexico would be a high-income country and immigration reform would not be a major issue in the United States. Weisbrot is codirector, Lefebvre a research assistant, and Sammut an intern at the Center for Economic and Policy Research, a progressive Washington, DC, think tank.

1. According to the authors, where does Mexico rank among Latin American countries in the growth of real GDP per person?
2. Weisbrot, Lefebvre, and Sammut claim that if NAFTA had been successful, Mexico's income per person would be significantly higher than which two countries?
3. What is the unemployment rate in Mexico, according to the authors?

I t is now 20 years [February 2014] since NAFTA [the North American Free Trade Agreement] went into effect, bringing Mexico into a new commercial agreement with the United States and Canada. At the time it was argued, and forecast, that the agreement would boost Mexico's growth and development.

NAFTA Has Not Helped Mexico's Economy

This [viewpoint] compares the performance of the Mexican economy with that of the rest of the region over the past 20 years, based on the available economic and social indicators, and with its own past economic performance. Among the results:

- Mexico ranks 18th of 20 Latin American countries in growth of real GDP per person, the most basic economic measure of living standards.

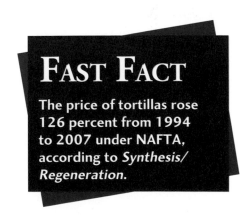

FAST FACT

The price of tortillas rose 126 percent from 1994 to 2007 under NAFTA, according to *Synthesis/ Regeneration.*

- From 1960–1980, Mexican real GDP per person almost doubled, growing by 98.7 percent. By comparison, in the past 20 years it has grown by just 18.6 percent.
- Mexico's per capita GDP growth of just 18.6 percent over the past 20 years is about half of the rate of growth achieved by the rest of Latin America.
- If NAFTA had been successful in restoring Mexico's pre-1980

growth rate—when developmentalist economic policies were the norm— Mexico today would be a relatively high income country, with income per person significantly higher than that of Portugal or Greece. It is unlikely that immigration reform would be a major political issue in the United States, since relatively few Mexicans would seek to cross the border.

- According to Mexican national statistics, Mexico's poverty rate of 52.3 percent in 2012 is almost identical to the poverty rate of 1994. As a result, there were 14.3 million more Mexicans living below the poverty line as of 2012 (the latest data available) than in 1994.
- We can use the poverty statistics of the UN Economic Commission on Latin America (ECLAC) to compare Mexico's poverty rate with the rest of Latin America. These statistics are computed differently and show a decline in poverty in Mexico. However, according to these measures, the rest of Latin America saw a drop in poverty that was more than two and a half times as much as that of Mexico: 20 percentage points (from 46 to 26 percent) for

Unemployed workers advertise their services on the side of a road in Mexico City. The unemployment rate in Mexico was higher in 2013 than when NAFTA was approved in 1994, leading some to conclude that NAFTA has had a negative effect on Mexico's labor force.

the rest of Latin America, versus 8 percentage points (from 45.1 to 37.1 percent) for Mexico.

- Real (inflation-adjusted) wages for Mexico were almost the same in 2012 as in 1994, up just 2.3 percent over 18 years, and barely above their level of 1980.
- Unemployment in Mexico is 5.0 percent today, as compared to an average of 3.1 percent for 1990–1994 and a low of 2.2 percent in 2000; these numbers seriously understate the true lack of jobs, but they show a significant deterioration in the labor market during the NAFTA years.
- NAFTA also had a severe impact on agricultural employment, as U.S. subsidized corn and other products wiped out family farmers in Mexico. From 1991–2007, there were 4.9 million Mexican family farmers displaced; while seasonal labor in agro-export industries increased by about 3 million. This meant a net loss of 1.9 million jobs.
- The very poor performance of the Mexican economy contributed to a surge in emigration to the United States. From 1994–2000, the annual number of Mexicans emigrating to the United States soared by 79 percent. The number of Mexican-born residents living in the United States more than doubled from 4.5 million in 1990 to 9.4 million in 2000, and peaked at 12.6 million in 2009.

NAFTA Led to Decades of Economic Failure

NAFTA was just one variable among others that could account for Mexico's poor economic performance over the past 20 years. However, it appears to be related to other economic policy choices that have negatively affected the Mexican economy during this period. The IMF notes that "Mexico competes directly with China in the U.S. market, where China accounts for 23 percent of U.S. imports and Mexico accounts for 12 percent." This is a very tough competition for Mexico for a number of reasons. First, Mexico was and remains a higher-wage country than China. . . . Mexico's exchange rate is unlikely to be competitive with China's, which further worsens its cost disadvantage. . . .

Average Annual Growth per Capita in Latin America, 1994–2013

Rank	Country	GDP Growth Rate
1	Panama	4.4%
2	Chile	3.4%
3	Peru	3.4%
4	Guyana	3.0%
5	Costa Rica	2.5%
6	Uruguay	2.5%
7	Argentina	2.5%
8	Suriname	2.4%
9	Colombia	2.1%
10	Nicaragua	2.0%
11	El Salvador	1.9%
12	Ecuador	1.9%
13	Brazil	1.8%
14	Bolivia	1.7%
15	Honduras	1.6%
16	Belize	1.5%
17	Paraguay	1.0%
18	**Mexico**	**0.9%**
19	Venezuela	0.8%
20	Guatemala	0.6%

Taken from: Mark Weisbrot, Stephan Lefebvre, and Joseph Sammut, "Did NAFTA Help Mexico?: An Assessment After 20 Years," Center for Economic and Policy Research, February 2014, p. 5.

China has other advantages that make it a formidable competitor for Mexico in the U.S. market: the Chinese government owns most of the banking system in China, and can therefore ensure that its most important exporting firms have sufficient access to credit. In Mexico, by contrast, 70 percent of the banking system is not only private but foreign-owned. . . .

NAFTA also increasingly tied Mexico to the U.S. economy, at a time when the U.S. economy was becoming dependent on growth driven by asset bubbles. As a result, Mexico suffered a recession when the stock market bubble burst in 2000–2002, and was one [of] the hardest hit countries in the region during the U.S. Great Recession, with a drop of 6.7 percent of GDP. . . .

As was well known at the time of NAFTA's passage, the main purpose of NAFTA was to lock in a set of economic policies, some of which were already well under way in the decade prior, including the liberalization of manufacturing, foreign investment and ownership, and other changes. The idea was that the continuation and expansion of these policies would allow Mexico to achieve efficiencies and economic progress that was not possible under the developmentalist, protectionist economic model that had prevailed in the decades before 1980. While some of the policy changes were undoubtedly necessary and/or positive, the end result has been decades of economic failure by almost any economic or social indicator. This is true whether we compare Mexico to its developmentalist past, or even if the comparison is to the rest of Latin America since NAFTA. After 20 years, these results should provoke more public discussion as to what went wrong.

EVALUATING THE AUTHORS' ARGUMENTS

In this viewpoint, Mark Weisbrot, Stephan Lefebvre, and Joseph Sammut argue that NAFTA has damaged Mexico's economic performance for the past twenty years. Who has the stronger argument about NAFTA's economic impact on Mexico in your opinion—the authors of this viewpoint or of the preceding viewpoint? Why?

In Middle of Mexico, a Middle Class Rises

Damien Cave

> "*Mexico is finally attracting the higher-end industries that experts say could lead to lasting prosperity.*"

In the following viewpoint, Damien Cave examines the growth of the middle class in Mexico. Cave maintains that a new economy in Mexico has emerged and that the nation is attracting higher-end industries that could lead to lasting prosperity. He profiles several members of the Mexican middle class and highlights the growing automotive industry. In order to maintain the country's growing middle class, the author contends, Mexico must make efforts to improve education, transform the energy sector, and prioritize innovation. Cave is a foreign correspondent for the *New York Times* based in Mexico City.

AS YOU READ, CONSIDER THE FOLLOWING QUESTIONS:
1. According to the author, what is the popular American conception of Mexico?
2. Cave claims that how many auto industry jobs have been added in Mexico since 2010?
3. What percentage of Mexicans between twenty-five and sixty-four have earned a high school degree, according to the author?

A decade ago, Ivan Zamora, 23, might have already left for the United States. Instead, he graduated in May [2013] from a gleaming new university here [Guanajuato, Mexico], then moved on to an engineering internship at one of the many multinational companies just beyond the campus gates.

His days now begin at dawn inside the new Volkswagen [VW] factory a short walk away, and when he leaves at night, he joins a rush of the upwardly mobile—from the cavernous new Pirelli plant next door, an array of Japanese car-parts suppliers and a new Nivea plant on a grassy hillside.

"There's just a lot more opportunity to study and to succeed," Mr. Zamora said at the factory, surrounded by robots, steel, glass and young technicians. "Both my parents are teachers. They lived in an entirely different era."

A New Mexico Has Emerged

Education. More sophisticated work. Higher pay. This is the development formula Mexico has been seeking for decades. But after the free-market wave of the 1990s failed to produce much more than low-skilled factory work, Mexico is finally attracting the higher-end industries that experts say could lead to lasting prosperity. Here, in a mostly poor state long known as one of the country's main sources of illegal immigrants to the United States, a new Mexico has begun to emerge.

Dozens of foreign companies are investing, filling in new industrial parks along the highways. Middle-class housing is popping up in former watermelon fields, and new universities are waving in classes of students eager to study engineering, aeronautics and biotechnology,

The University of Guanajuato is part of Mexico's public university system. Mexico has seen an increase in its middle-class population partly because of an emphasis on higher education as a way to succeed.

signaling a growing confidence in Mexico's economic future and what many see as the imported meritocracy of international business. In a country where connections and corruption are still common tools of enrichment, many people here are beginning to believe they can get ahead through study and hard work.

Mr. Zamora's new job, for example (he was hired by VW at summer's end), started with his parents prioritizing education, not emigration, and scrimping to give him a computer and, more recently, German lessons. The state of Guanajuato added to their investment by building the affordable polytechnic—part of a public university system that offers tech-

nical degrees as well as undergraduate and graduate degrees—and a sprawling interior port to lure the international companies that hire its graduates. And now Mr. Zamora has a job that pays enough to help his sister pursue her dream of studying marine biology.

This is a Mexico far different from the popular American conception: it is neither the grinding, low-skilled assembly work at maquiladoras, the multinational factories near the border, nor the ugliness of drug cartels. But the question many experts and officials are asking is whether Mexico as a whole can keep up with the rising demand for educated labor—and overcome concerns about crime and corruption—to propel its 112 million people into the club of developed nations.

"We are at something of a turning point," said Eric Verhoogen, a professor of economics and international affairs at Columbia University. "The maquila strategy has been revealed not to have been successful, so people are looking around for something new."

A Growing Automotive Industry

The automotive industry has been Mexico's brightest spot so far. In many ways, central Mexico has already surpassed Detroit. There are now more auto-industry jobs in Mexico than in the entire American

Rising Educational Attainment in Mexico

The number of students receiving a higher education in Mexico has tripled since 1980.

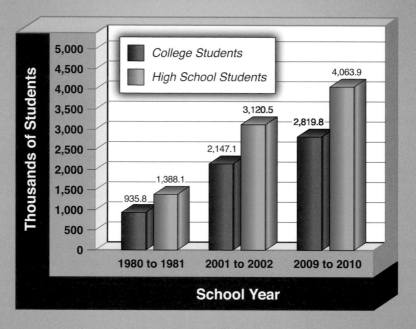

Taken from: Luis de la Calle and Luis Rubio, *Mexico: A Middle Class Society, Poor No More, Developed Not Yet.* Washington, DC: Woodrow Wilson International Center for Scholars, 2012, p. 44.

Midwest. At least 100,000 jobs have been added in Mexico since 2010, according to a recent Brookings Institution report, and General Motors, Ford, Chrysler, Honda, Mazda, Nissan, Audi and Volkswagen have all announced expansion plans, with nearly $10 billion to be invested over the next several years, mainly in a 400-mile corridor from Puebla to Aguascalientes.

The work tends to be better paid than what could be found in the area before the companies arrived. It is still a fraction of the salaries of American workers—many employees on the factory floors in the interior port make around $3.65 an hour—but higher-paid professionals make up about 30 percent of the employees at many auto plants here, roughly twice as much as in the maquiladoras near the border.

And although robotics and other changes have kept overall employment in the industry somewhat limited, more of the industry has moved to Mexico as the car business has recovered. Around 40 percent of all auto-industry jobs in North America are in Mexico, up from 27 percent in 2000 (the Midwest has about 30 percent), and experts say the growth is accelerating, especially in Guanajuato, where state officials have been increasing incentives.

The 2,600-acre interior port, for example, has become a draw because, in addition to the polytechnic, the state built customs facilities, a railroad depot and a link to the local airport. Guanajuato also helps find candidates for companies to hire and, in some cases, gives them free classes to help them pass standardized tests required for employment. At Volkswagen, many of the young men and women flowing in and out of test-taking sessions said they benefited from the assistance.

An Expanding Middle Class

Guanajuato even pays companies a small bonus for sending workers abroad for training. Mauricio Martínez, 29, an engineer at the Italian tiremaker Pirelli, which was one of the first companies to take up residence in the port, said he and his wife, Mariana, still saw their trip to Prague after his training in Romania as a fairy tale.

"I'm a small-town guy," he said one day after work, in his kitchen with a beer. "But there I was; an Italian company from Milan hired a small-town guy from Mexico."

He said he now makes $2,250 a month ($27,000 a year), far more than at his old job at a tow-truck company and roughly double the median household income nationwide. That's more than enough for a middle-class life here. Both husband and wife drive to work, and this year they bought a three-bedroom townhouse in a new development for about $80,000. On a recent visit, "The Big Bang Theory" played on their flat-screen TV as a neighbor watered her patch of lawn no bigger than a beach towel.

While cooking dinner, Mrs. Martínez said that her husband's job had given them the credit and stability they needed to start her own business—a gourmet salad shop in a colonial village nearby. And as is common in other countries with an expanding middle class, such as Brazil, their economic rise has led to demands for better government.

When someone recently stole Mrs. Martínez's cellphone, she said she went straight to the police over the objections of her father, who warned her nothing would be done. "He was right," she said. "But next time it happens, I want my complaint to be there. I'm trying to make a living here, and I want a legal life."

"My generation, we're more prepared," she added. "My parents, they never even finished school; we know if something is going to change, it has to start with us."

Meeting the Demand for Skilled Employees

Many young, middle-class Mexicans are coming to similar realizations, propelled by 13 years of democracy and the Internet. But their ranks are small. As the auto industry rebounds and wage inflation in China makes Mexico more attractive for global manufacturers, many foreign employers say that skilled employees are harder to find and

Customers shop at a Costco near Mexico City in 2012. Businesses such as Walmart and Costco are opening in many parts of the nation to service the growing population of middle-class Mexicans.

keep, while the mass of Mexican workers do not measure up to what many companies need.

Only 36 percent of Mexicans between 25 and 64 have earned the equivalent of a high school degree, according to the Organization for Economic Cooperation and Development. Despite a rapid rise in foreign investment, with 2013 shaping up to be Mexico's best year on record, the country is still struggling.

The Mexican economy has slowed significantly this year, and even when it was doing better, the nation's poverty rate fell only 0.6 percent to 53.3 million people—roughly 45 percent of the population—between 2010 and 2012. Crime and a notoriously weak justice system continue to undermine the economy, with Mexico's minister of health recently estimating that it costs 1.34 percent of the country's annual gross domestic product. "It's all the stuff we hear about again and again: Mexico has an education system that is not on par with its peers; a banking system that's not lending; it has rule-of-law issues and public-security issues and corruption being a huge issue," said Christopher Wilson, an economics scholar at the Woodrow Wilson International Center for Scholars in Washington [DC]. "The list goes on and on."

Prioritizing Education and Innovation

Many economists and business consultants are keeping a close watch on President Enrique Peña Nieto's efforts to improve education, open the energy sector to private investment and overhaul taxes.

Kevin P. Gallagher, an economist at Boston University, said Mexico also needed to prioritize innovation. "South Korea and Taiwan spend over 2 percent of G.D.P. on research and development; China spends almost 2 percent," he said. "Mexico spends 0.4 percent."

But on a smaller scale in Guanajuato, individual success is creating a sense of possibility. Some of Mr. Zamora's friends are studying German, too, hoping to land work at Volkswagen, and a similar sense of momentum pervades the polytechnic, where students in pristine industrial labs, like Javier Eduardo Luna Zapata, 24, have begun to dream of more than work at an auto plant.

He and a few classmates won a prestigious design award this year for a scanner that would check airport runways for debris. "We want to start a company," he said, displaying a video of the project on his cellphone. "We're going to look for investors when we graduate."

His classmates, representing a new generation of Mexicans—mostly geeks in jeans carrying smartphones—all nodded with approval.

EVALUATING THE AUTHOR'S ARGUMENTS

In this viewpoint, Damien Cave claims that the Mexican middle class is rising and a new economy in Mexico has emerged. Explain how someone might argue that Mexico is not becoming a middle-class nation.

As Mexico Claws Toward Prosperity, Some in Middle Class Slide Back

"Many middle-class Mexicans are barely making it."

William Booth and Nick Miroff

In the following viewpoint, William Booth and Nick Miroff examine the emerging middle class in Mexico. While the economy is growing, the authors maintain that life is still extremely fragile for most members of Mexico's middle class. The authors highlight the impact of organized crime, persistent levels of income disparity, the need for education reform, and the lack of structural support for small business owners. The authors argue that Mexico is still far from completing its transformation from a mostly poor country into a more competitive nation. Booth and Miroff are correspondents for the *Washington Post*.

Thirty years ago [as of December 2012], Lourdes Huesca and her husband moved to a tiny patch of land in the muddy bean fields at the edge of Mexico City. The young couple lived in a shack, with no water or electricity, in the poor, rural, old Mexico.

Huesca, who never learned to read but could add numbers in her head, marched her sons to the schoolhouse every day. The family struggled, sacrificed, saved.

A generation later, the family owns a shoe stall in the market and a nice cement-block home with three bedrooms, landscape oil paintings on the wall, and a new flat-screen TV, a gift from the eldest son, an environmental systems engineer.

"Mexico has given me so much," Huesca said.

But she knows how easy it would be for her family to fall back down again in a country where social mobility too often moves in the wrong direction.

FAST FACT

According to *Forbes*, while Mexico's top income group saw a 4.5 percent increase in income between 2010 and 2012, many middle-income families saw their household income drop.

A Fragile Middle Class

By a wide range of social and economic indicators, Mexico has reached a turning point, development experts say. The country is no longer poor, though it is a long way from being rich. Huesca and a narrow majority of Mexico's 114 million citizens have clawed their way into an emerging middle class.

The changes are transforming Mexico's relationship with the United States. The once-wary neighbors are now top trading partners, with more than $1 billion in goods crossing the border each day. Together, Mexican and U.S. workers manufacture automobiles, airplanes, computers and space satellites.

A more solidly middle-class and open Mexico is also providing a close-to-home market for U.S. goods and services, while contributing to a reduction in the number of underemployed Mexicans heading north to work illegally in the United States.

But in fundamental ways, Mexico is still far from completing its transformation from a mostly poor country of low wages and low expectations into a richer, better-educated and more competitive nation, a modern success story.

Many middle-class Mexicans are barely making it.

Huesca, 53, is healthy, but her husband has diabetes, and because the couple worked in the informal economy all their lives, they have no health insurance, no social security. When they go to the doctor, they pay cash. They have no pensions, no savings and no assets, except the family home on a dirt street.

Two of their sons have graduated from college. A third is finishing up at a public university. But if anyone in the family loses a job, or gets seriously ill, Huesca could quickly join the 3 million Mexicans who slid from the middle class back into poverty during the last recession.

About 17 percent of Mexicans joined the ranks of the middle class from 2000 to 2010, according to a recent World Bank report, and though the traditionally wide gap between country's rich and poor persists, measures of inequality among citizens fell more in Mexico than in any other Latin American country, except Peru.

Addressing Income Disparity

But Mexico—with the 13th-largest economy in the world, built on booming free trade with the United States—still functions far below its competitors, according to analysis by its own leaders in the World Bank and the Organization for Economic Cooperation and Development (OECD), a club of 34 developed countries.

In Mexico, middle-class workers earn an income closer to the wages at the bottom than the top. Disparity is great. The bottom 10 percent receives just 1.3 percent of total income, while the top 10 percent receives 36 percent.

The nation's relatively anemic growth and lingering inequalities—compared with regional rivals such as Brazil and Chile, or economic rivals such as South Korea and Turkey—condemn millions to a tenacious poverty that hangs like an anchor around Mexico's neck.

The country's new president, Enrique Peña Nieto vows to raise 15 million people from poverty in the next six years by tripling economic growth, providing loans to small and medium businesses, and tearing down the walls that have insulated monopolies and the elite from competition.

It is an ambitious agenda, one that his predecessor, Felipe Calderon, never achieved in a term during which poverty rose as the 2009 global economic crisis took its toll, despite soaring public spending on social welfare programs. . . .

Mexico's struggle to secure a better future is plain to see in edge cities such as Chalco, no longer a slum but not quite the suburbs, where ordinary families tell of how hard it is to make it in Mexico.

The Chalco Valley, once the shoreline of a shallow lake fished by Aztec vassals, was a sleepy dairy pasture for most of the 20th century.

A teacher leads a class at an elementary school in Nayarit, Mexico. Experts argue that Mexico's economic improvements will stall if it does not improve its failing education system.

After the devastating Mexico City earthquake of 1985, refugees from the capital turned a backwater into a gritty, mercantile metropolis.

Now the Chalco Valley is home to 850,000 residents and is filled with new schools, clinics and playgrounds built by the government, with Wal-Marts and AutoZones rising from cement-block barrios that 25 years ago lacked running water.

"In 1976, there were two primary schools in Chalco," said Mayor Esteban Hernandez. "Today, we have 380 schools, including six universities."

Education Has Changed Mexican Society

The mayor said education, more than anything else, has changed the fortunes of Mexico. "If the kids can go to school," Hernandez said, "then the mother can work, and the family income rises, and the child gets an education."

Mexico can afford to educate more children because its population is no longer exploding. The nation's fertility rate in the 1960s was seven children per mother; today, it is two per mother.

Lourdes Huesca came from a family of 10 siblings. But she and her husband have only three sons, "and to me, that's a lot," she said.

"I told my sons they were going to get an education," Huesca said.

All three went to college.

Her youngest is enrolled at the National Polytechnic Institute, the "MIT of Mexico," where tuition, books and bus fare cost the family about $200 a semester. He wants to be a computer engineer.

"Once my third son finishes his studies," Huesca said, "my life will be complete."

Her children are the exception.

Nearly all Mexican children ages 5 to 14 are in school, a tremendous advance. But only 20 percent of 25- to 34-year-olds have gotten a college education, compared with 37 percent across other OECD countries.

According to surveys of school principals, 70 percent of Mexican teachers—who belong to one of the most powerful unions in Latin America, run by a boss with lifetime tenure—arrive to work late, are not prepared for their classes or routinely fail to show up.

The Other Economy

Mexico's illicit economy—including a thriving black market—is still the fastest way forward for many, reflecting a rampant criminality that drags the country down.

Eva Ortiz has made a decent middle-class life for her family by selling pirated DVDs in the Chalco market. Orphaned as an infant, she was a maid at age 10, an abuse victim at 14 and a mother at 15.

She didn't spend a single day of her childhood in a classroom.

Instead, she began selling bootleg VHS tapes of Disney cartoons. Few Mexicans see the trade as anything to be ashamed about—though the Motion Picture Association of America says piracy costs its members $300 million to $600 million a year in lost revenue in Mexico.

Today, Ortiz is Chalco's best-known purveyor of movies and video games. She employs three clerks. "People here can't afford to spend 100 pesos [$8] to buy these movies in a store," said Ortiz, 39, who sells them for a dollar each.

She benefits from illegality—but pays a price.

So does Mexico.

The Impact of Crime on Mexican Society

Transparency International ranks the country a low 105 of 174 nations in its annual Corruption Perceptions Index, behind Jamaica, China, Bulgaria. The group says a motorist's likelihood of bribing a traffic cop in Mexico state, where Chalco is located (and where Peña Nieto was governor) is more than 80 percent.

Ortiz has sold enough bootleg copies to afford a 2009 Chevy SUV and a cement-block home for her four daughters.

But on three occasions last year, Mexican federal police raided the market and confiscated thousands of dollars' worth of her merchandise.

Because Mexico's drug cartels control a major portion of the illegal DVD trade, Ortiz's cash business in the black market has left her vulnerable.

Armed men broke into her house three years ago, she said, holding her daughter at gunpoint until she withdrew her life savings from the bank—money she had set aside for a home in a safer neighborhood.

Bribery in Mexico

Likelihood of bribing traffic police when stopped to avoid being fined or detained:

Note: Based on a survey by Transparency International of 15,000 Mexican homes on bribery.

Taken from: "Bribery in Mexico: Contrasting Corruption," *The Economist*, May 20, 2011. www.economist.com.

Although the sensational violence associated with drug trafficking grabs international headlines, it is the other crime wave that most upsets Mexicans.

There were a record number of auto thefts last year: More than 85,000 cars were stolen. Robbery has increased 45 percent from 2005 to early 2012. Extortion is now the most reported crime in half of Mexico—an estimated 4.4 million attempts last year. Yet the federal census bureau found that only 12 percent of crimes are reported, because Mexicans don't trust the police. Only 8 percent are investigated.

"My life has been difficult ever since I was kid," Ortiz said. More bad luck followed. She received a diagnosis of cancer in the summer.

Ortiz is one of 14 million Mexicans—one-third of the labor force, and growing—who work in the informal sector.

Paid in cash and off the books, they and their employers skirt taxes and fail to enroll in government social security programs.

Ortiz has no health insurance, and she can't afford to take time away from her DVDs. "I can't get ahead if I don't work," she said, biting her lip and worrying for her daughters. "I'm the one who keeps my family together."

Small-Business Owners Struggle to Survive

A few blocks from where Ortiz hawks the latest James Bond movie, Miguel Nieves sells his elaborate cakes, decorated to celebrate birthdays and weddings.

"When I was a kid, we didn't have enough to eat sometimes. We didn't have our own house or a car," Nieves said. "We never took a vacation."

But Nieves, 38, earned an engineering degree and an MBA, then applied his business management training to his mother's recipes. Twenty years later, he has three bakeries and 16 employees.

"Now I have a visa to go to the U.S. whenever I want," he said. "No problems."

Nieves said it is especially hard for small-business owners in Mexico to get ahead. He wants to open a fourth pastry shop and hire more workers, but affordable credit is impossible to come by.

His bank offered him a commercial loan at steep rates, starting at 25 percent. Credit card interest rates, plus fees, can top 50 percent.

"There's no financing here," Nieves said. "I have to save everything myself, and if you can't save, you can't grow."

Mexican banks have more than quadrupled the amount of money available for credit since 1994, according to Bank of Mexico, and the number of credit cards in circulation has soared from 6 million to

25 million in the past decade. But economists say access to affordable credit remains one of the biggest impediments to growth.

In response, the banks—mostly foreign-owned—say Mexican courts are dysfunctional and don't protect loan guarantees, so lenders have to charge high rates to cover defaults.

Nieves said he still has "a lot of confidence" in Mexico's future. But he sees a business climate stacked against entrepreneurs like himself who play by the rules.

He has seen his home town transformed. But he said it is not yet a middle-class place.

"You have to be ambitious," he said. "You can't be satisfied with what you have. We still lack a culture that says, 'I want more.'"

EVALUATING THE AUTHORS' ARGUMENTS

In this viewpoint, William Booth and Nick Miroff claim that many societal issues in Mexico threaten the emerging middle class. Whose perspective on the state of the middle class in Mexico is more convincing in your opinion—that of the authors of this viewpoint or that of Damien Cave? Why?

Chapter 2

What Are Mexico's Greatest Challenges and Opportunities?

A group of crosses near the US border in El Sásabe, Mexico, tries to discourage people from making the often deadly crossing through the Sonoran desert into Arizona. Large numbers of Mexicans brave extremely dangerous situations to flee poverty and lack of opportunity at home.

Mexico Must Combat Corruption

"Discontent with the government's chronic failure in eradicating corruption and establishing the rule of law in Mexico has reached new highs."

Rodrigo Aguilera

In the following viewpoint, Rodrigo Aguilera argues that corruption is the major challenge affecting Mexican society. Many hoped that the establishment of democracy in 2000 would reduce corruption; however, Aguilera states that Mexico has been unable to fight corruption on either a local or a national level. This has led to discontent among the public and prevented the nation from becoming successful, he contends. Aguilera is Latin American editor and economist for the Economist Intelligence Unit, a research branch of the global publication *The Economist*.

AS YOU READ, CONSIDER THE FOLLOWING QUESTIONS:

1. According to the author, what event in 2000 did Mexicans believe would lead to the strengthening of the rule of law?
2. What did Mexican president Enrique Peña Nieto announce as one his first initiatives, according to the author?

Ask the experts what they think the root of Mexico's problems is and you'll get a myriad of responses: an economy that despite its export success, suffers from big local monopolies which stifle internal competition; the inability to achieve a sustainable reduction in poverty and inequality even during periods of growth; an education system hijacked by its notoriously powerful union; the dominance of organized crime groups significantly impairing governability; a political system that is notoriously inflexible and subject to chronic legislative paralysis. However, ask the average Mexican the same question, and the answer will most likely be corruption.

The experts may be right on the details but in a broader sense, it's hard to think of any other issue that, besides corruption, has had such a toxic pervasiveness in Mexican society. Unfortunately, hopes that the establishment of democracy in 2000 would inevitably lead to the strengthening of the rule of law have fallen short.

Fighting Corruption

Discontent with the government's chronic failure in eradicating corruption and establishing the rule of law in Mexico has reached new highs amid the surge in drug-related violence since 2007. It has also been highlighted more recently by the allegations of fraud against the PRI [Institutional Revolutionary Party], following the July 1st [2012] victory of its candidate, Enrique Peña Nieto, in the general election. Although small-scale electoral fraud is not uncommon in Latin America, Mexico appears unique among the region's established democracies in having not one but two straight presidential elections legally challenged by the opposition. With the PRI keen on presenting itself as a renovated political force, it was not surprising therefore, that Peña Nieto announced an anti-corruption bill as one of his first initiatives.

The bill, sent to Congress on November 14th, seeks to create an anti-corruption commission (Comisión Nacional Anticorrupción or CNA) which will be tasked with investigating corruption cases at a

Allegations of corruption in the 2012 presidential election of Enrique Peña Nieto sparked protests such as the Yo Soy 132 movement across Mexico.

federal level and against individuals. It will also have the ability to tackle cases at a state and municipal level, but only if they have national repercussions. Crucially, the commission will be able to sidestep legal hurdles such as bank and fiscal secrecy which would, in theory, make it a powerful tool against money laundering. In order to avoid duplication of roles, the existing Secretaría de Función Pública (a public administration ministry) would be eliminated, and its current duties shared between the CNA and the treasury.

Questioning the PRI's Commitment

In creating this new commission, Peña Nieto's team appears inspired by the success of other developing countries in setting up similar institutions, such as Indonesia and Georgia which has been reflected in

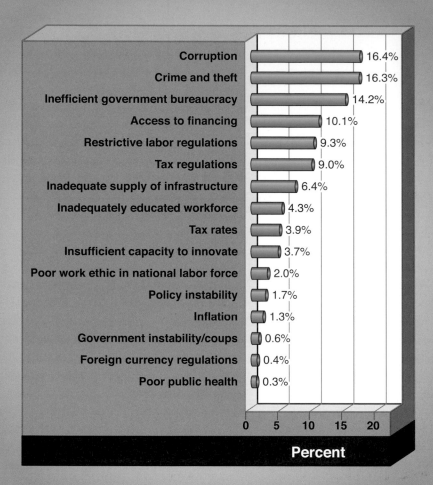

The Most Problematic Factors for Doing Business in Mexico

Factor	Percent
Corruption	16.4%
Crime and theft	16.3%
Inefficient government bureaucracy	14.2%
Access to financing	10.1%
Restrictive labor regulations	9.3%
Tax regulations	9.0%
Inadequate supply of infrastructure	6.4%
Inadequately educated workforce	4.3%
Tax rates	3.9%
Insufficient capacity to innovate	3.7%
Poor work ethic in national labor force	2.0%
Policy instability	1.7%
Inflation	1.3%
Government instability/coups	0.6%
Foreign currency regulations	0.4%
Poor public health	0.3%

Percent

Note: Based on World Economic Forum Executive Opinion Survey conducted between January and June 2012. From the list of factors above, respondents were asked to select and rank the five most problematic for doing business in their country. The bars in the figure show the responses weighted according to their rankings.

Taken from: Klaus Schwab, "The Global Competitiveness Report 2012–2013," World Economic Forum, 2012, p. 256.

the significant jumps they have made in Transparency International's Corruption Perception Index (CPI) over the past few years. However, there is reason to fear that Mexico's CNA, as currently envisioned, will struggle to replicate this success.

First of all, Mexico's track record on institutional development—be it in creating new institutions or reforming existing ones—is disappointing. For example, its competition bodies, such as the Cofeco and Cofetel have been shown to be toothless, as witnessed by their failure in standing up to the big domestic monopolies. The IFAI [Federal Institute for Access to Public Information] has given an important boost to federal-level transparency, but similar bodies on a state-level (where opacity is even more pervasive) have been slow to set up. The all too frequent establishment and then disbandment of federal police forces (the latest victim being the AFI [Mexico's former federal investigation agency]) is a further proof that the problem of creating trustworthy and efficient institutions goes further than simply changing name and logo.

FAST FACT

In a 2013 survey by Transparency International, 80 percent of respondents in Mexico felt that the judiciary was corrupt or extremely corrupt.

Second and perhaps most important, is that the PRI's commitment to fighting corruption appears rather hollow, given the sheer number of scandals its state governors have faced over the past decade, the electoral controversy, and the recent negotiation on the labor reform bill. During the latter, the PRI's legislators essentially sabotaged a number of key clauses which attempted to introduce transparency and democratic practices to the unions. That the corruption bill was introduced by the PRI at the very same time that its legislators were making their final efforts at maintaining the status quo for one of Mexico's most powerful interest groups, speaks volumes about the party's willingness to stamp out corruption among its closest allies—let alone within its ranks. Crucially, the CNA's five commissioners are to be appointed by the executive, casting a serious doubt over its independence.

Can Mexico Be Successful Despite Corruption?

Contrary to conventional wisdom, the economic evidence appears to show that countries can be corrupt and successful at the same time. So why not Mexico? Unlike countries such as China and (to a lesser extent) Brazil, Mexico's recent administrations have appeared woefully lacking in ambition, showing neither the power nor the will to impose their agenda. And unlike low-income India, Mexico's middle-income economy does not have the convergence potential which would allow it such rapid growth.

Even then, it should be noted that Mexico actually ranked below these three countries in Transparency International's latest CPI, and also ranked a dreadful second worst among Latin America's "big seven" (only behind Venezuela). According to the latest WEF [World Economic Forum] Global Competitiveness Report, corruption was the single most problematic factor in doing business in Mexico. For China it was only the fifth, and for Brazil, a distant seventh. It is clear that in Mexico, corruption matters, and it will take more than a new commission to raise hope that the rule of law will reign supreme anytime soon.

EVALUATING THE AUTHOR'S ARGUMENTS

In this viewpoint, Rodrigo Aguilera claims that corruption is the major societal ill preventing Mexico from becoming a successful country. Do you agree with the author's argument, or do you believe that another issue in Mexico presents more of a challenge? Explain your answer.

Mexico Must Combat Human Rights Abuses

"Mexico continues to face serious challenges to the rule of law and respect for human rights."

Amnesty International

In the following viewpoint, Amnesty International urges Mexican president Enrique Peña Nieto to address the human rights issues affecting his country. The organization highlights reports of human rights abuses committed by police and security forces, such as enforced disappearances, torture, and arbitrary detention. The author contends that human rights defenders and journalists face increasing attacks. The justice system continues to fail society, the organization argues, and the government has not responded to this critical situation. Amnesty International is a global nongovernmental organization that works against the abuse of human rights.

AS YOU READ, CONSIDER THE FOLLOWING QUESTIONS:

1. What type of human rights abuses in Mexico does Amnesty International highlight?
2. According to the author, what is the most important change to Mexico's legal framework in decades?

Mexico continues to face serious challenges to the rule of law
and respect for human rights. The alarming security situation in many parts of the country and the consequences of
militarized combat of organized crime and drug cartels, initiated by
the previous administration [Felipe Calderón], has increased insecurity
and violence in many regions, leaving many communities unprotected
and at risk from all sides of the conflict. Reports of human rights
abuses committed by police and security forces, including enforced
disappearances, torture and arbitrary detention continue and impunity for all crimes remains the norm. Human rights defenders and
journalists, who often try to support victims and expose abuses, face
increasing attacks. Women, indigenous peoples and migrants face
discrimination and violence, but their chances of redress are slim. The
justice system continues to fail victims, accused and society. These are
just some of the human rights problems that people have to face in
their daily lives, but so far the government has not responded to this
critical situation. . . .

Amnesty International's experience around the world has shown
that when a government wants to really change the prevailing culture
of human rights abuses and impunity, it must demonstrate that it is
prepared to make this a real political priority and not pay mere lip-
service to international human rights commitments; making clear that
officials can no longer ignore or relegate human rights to the slow lane.
Above all, in order to show that impunity will no longer be tolerated,
it must demonstrate in practice that anyone implicated directly or
indirectly in human rights abuses will face justice and victims will
have access to truth and reparations. Amnesty International urges the
President [Enrique Peña Nieto] and his cabinet to show this strong
determination and commitment to address the critical human rights
situation in the country.

In this context, Amnesty International would like to raise a number
of pressing concerns about the human rights situation in Mexico and
to make a series of recommendations to President Peña Nieto and his
administration:

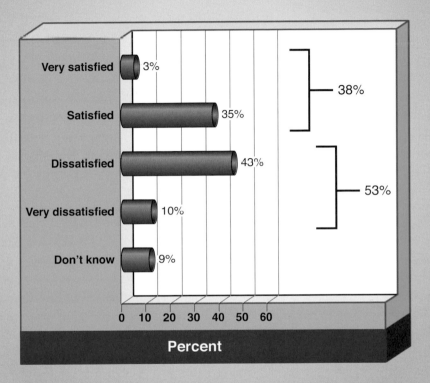

Are you very satisfied, satisfied, dissatisfied, or very dissatisfied with the Mexican government's actions to defend and protect the human rights of people in Mexico?

Very satisfied — 3%

Satisfied — 35%

Dissatisfied — 43%

Very dissatisfied — 10%

Don't know — 9%

38%

53%

Percent

Note: Based on a national survey of 800 households conducted between September 28 and October 2, 2013.

Taken from: Parametría, "Derechos Humanos Conocidos pero Poco Respetados en México" ("Human Rights Recognized but Not Widely Respected in Mexico"), 2013. www.parametria.com.mx.

Human Rights Reforms

The 2011 constitutional human rights reform is potentially the most important change to Mexico's legal framework in decades. It provides a vital mechanism for upholding international human rights standards in national law, but as yet the government and legislature have failed to adopt implementing legislation or send a clear message that international human rights standards will be enforced in practice.

The government must establish a legislative agenda in consultation with civil society to fully incorporate constitutional human rights reforms into domestic legislation at every level.

Public Security and Human Rights

It is no surprise that Michoacán state is the most visible example of the ongoing public security crisis. The state which witnessed the start of the ill-fated militarized combat of organized crime has endured years of violence and insecurity at the hands of criminal gangs as well as police and security forces, some of whom operate in collusion with criminal gangs. Self-defence groups appear to be a response to this neglect and abuse, but themselves now test the State's willingness to meet security and human rights obligations. The challenge for the present administration is to rebuild the social fabric and forge institutions which the population can trust and that do not resort to human rights violations. It is one thing to affirm that human rights are respected in public security policy, another is to really ensure that credible accountability mechanisms are in place to detect and uphold these standards, including to prevent and punish any abuses committed by self-defence groups. So far there is no evidence that the government is prepared to ensure that this is the case and make a clear break with the practices of the previous government. In other states like Veracruz, Tamaulipas, Coahuila, Chihuahua and Guerrero, where violence, insecurity and human rights violations remain a daily threat to local populations, they receive little attention of policy makers or media.

The government must ensure all police and security forces, as well as self-defence groups, respect international human rights norms on the use of force and prohibiting other human rights violations.

The president should take every opportunity to send a strong public message that abuses will not be tolerated. He should direct that all allegations of noncompliance with international norms on the use of force or other human rights be immediately, exhaustively, and impartially investigated, with the perpetrators brought to justice and victims receiving full reparations.

Disappearances, Torture, and Ill-Treatment

A year on from the government making public the database of more than 26,000 people reported disappeared or missing during the last administration, the government has yet to publish a revised database of those people who remain victims of abduction by criminal gangs or enforced disappearances in which public officials are implicated. The promised national database of disappeared persons remains inoperative. . . .

When, as presidential candidate, Enrique Peña Nieto told Amnesty International that he assumed "the clear commitment to implement policies and actions to eradicate any act of torture" . . . the organization hoped that this would be the first serious step to acknowledging the true scale of torture and ill-treatment used by security forces and police at all levels in Mexico. However, torture and ill-treatment are rife. Most existing preventive measures appear more designed to under-record levels of torture and ill-treatment and ensure perpetrators avoid justice. As a result, the criminal justice system continues to rely on torture as the primary means of investigation. . . .

FAST FACT

Mexico's special prosecutor for crimes against journalists says that sixty-seven journalists were killed and fourteen disappeared in the country between 2006 and 2012.

Criminal Justice System

The criminal justice system remains the nexus of many of Mexico's human rights problems. Arbitrary detentions, fabricated criminal charges, denial of due process and fair trial remain routine and all too rarely exposed and remedied. Arraigo detentions, which allow prosecutors to detain suspects for long periods in order to conduct investigations, continue to encourage abuses and undermine judicial supervision. The repeated recommendations of international human rights mechanisms to abolish arraigo detentions have been ignored. It is assumed that judicial reform—started in 2008 but introduced in only a handful of states ahead of the 2016 deadline—will improve the rights of victims and defendants and will produce better judicial decisions. However, in states that have introduced such reforms, like Chihuahua, statements obtained under torture have been ruled admissible, subverting human rights protections the new procedural system is supposed to safeguard. The unified procedural code recently approved by Congress for federal and state criminal jurisdictions must avoid this and ensure that illegally obtained evidence, such as statements extracted under torture, are not admitted as evidence and other due process guarantees are respected. It must also ensure the end of impunity for public officials implicated in human rights violations.

Ensure effective and impartial investigation and prosecution of all allegations of torture and other ill-treatment. Acts of torture and other ill-treatment must be prosecuted as such rather than under lesser charges, such as "abuse of authority."

Ensure that any official who fails to record evidence of torture or ill-treatment is held to account.

Review medical examination procedures to ensure that anyone reporting torture or ill-treatment is immediately examined in line with the UN Istanbul Protocol and ensure that independent medical evaluations in line with this standard are accepted as evidence in judicial proceedings.

Strictly enforce the rule that evidence obtained as the result of torture is inadmissible in court.

The government must take steps to abolish "arraigo" and ensure that all detentions are lawful and are accurately recorded on an accessible national database.

Military Justice

Members of the army and navy continue to be implicated in grave human rights violations such as torture, extrajudicial killings and enforced disappearance. The National Supreme Court compliance with Inter American Court of Human Rights judgements requiring Mexico to exclude human rights crimes from military jurisdiction is a crucial step in making justice accessible to the victims and their relatives. Amnesty International welcomes the Senate's recent decision to remove the reservation to the article of the Inter-American Convention on the Forced Disappearance of Persons which prohibits

In Mexico City hundreds of relatives of missing people participate in the 2014 March of Dignity, organized by Amnesty International to protest and demand justice from the Mexican government.

the application of military jurisdiction in cases of enforced disappearance. It is also welcome that military authorities are declining judicial competence in some cases in favour of the civilian justice system. Yet the government and the legislature have so far failed to comply with the same IACHR sentences requiring the reform of the Code of Military Justice. As a result there is legal uncertainty regarding jurisdiction, particularly during initial investigations of alleged human rights crimes committed by military personnel.

Reform the code of military justice to ensure that all allegations of human rights violations committed by military personnel are investigated, prosecuted and tried in the civilian justice system.

Irregular Migrants

In 2013, 82,269 migrants were detained by migration authorities in Mexico and 75,704 were deported, the vast majority to Guatemala, Honduras and El Salvador. Far more Central American migrants tried to make the journey to the USA. In Mexico many migrants continue to suffer abuses at the hands of police and others are the victims of targeted kidnapping, trafficking, rape and killing by criminal gangs which often operate in collusion with local authorities. . . .

Human Rights Defenders and Journalists

Human rights defenders and journalists face attacks, threats, intimidation and abduction and killing in reprisal for their legitimate and vital work. Those behind the attacks are almost never brought to justice. . . .

Women's Human Rights

Despite government measures to support women's rights, gender equality remains a far-off goal. Violence and discrimination against women and girls violate their human rights and severely compromise their sexual and reproductive health and rights. . . .

Indigenous People's Rights

Twenty years after the emergence of the Ejército Zapatista de Liberación Nacional (EZLN) in Chiapas, many indigenous communities across the country continue to face discrimination, including limited access to justice, health, education, housing and land. The measures taken by the government so far do not adequately address many of the major structural obstacles to the enjoyment of these rights.

EVALUATING THE AUTHOR'S ARGUMENTS

In this viewpoint, Amnesty International urges the Peña Nieto administration to take a more active approach to human rights issues in Mexico. According to the organization, what actions should the government take to combat civil rights abuses in Mexico? Do you agree? Why or why not?

Improving the Mexican Economy Would Decrease Illegal Immigration to the United States

"The economic conditions in both Mexico and the United States are key determinants in people's migration."

Guillermo Cantor

In the following viewpoint, Guillermo Cantor examines a trend of immigrants' returning to Mexico from the United States voluntarily. Cantor maintains that economic factors such as the US recession as well as immigration policy play a role in this trend. He argues that the United States has failed to understand the complexity of international migration. In order to fight unauthorized immigration from Mexico, the author maintains, the policy makers in the United States must create a more flexible system for legal immigration and cooperate with Mexico to ensure that economic prosperity in Mexico is a reality. Cantor is a senior analyst at the American Immigration Council's Immigration Policy Center.

AS YOU READ, CONSIDER THE FOLLOWING QUESTIONS:

1. According to the author, how many people moved from the United States to Mexico between 2005 and 2010?
2. What does Cantor believe caused the reversal in the net migration flow between Mexico and the United States?
3. Why should policy makers in the United States pay attention to the findings of the MATT study, according to the author?

Mexicans and Americans Thinking Together (MATT) has presented[1] the results of a new study[2] that highlights some recent, significant shifts in return migration from the United States to Mexico. One of the merits of this study is that it reminds us of the dynamic and bi-directional nature of migratory flows between the two countries. Between 2005 and 2010, 1.39

Demonstrators protest US immigration policies at a 2010 rally in Los Angeles, California. Some argue that improvements to the Mexican economy would greatly reduce the number of immigrants from Mexico to the United States.

million people moved from the U.S. to Mexico, of whom 985,000 were returning migrants. Interestingly, deportations (which, as we know, have escalated tremendously[3] during the [US president Barack] Obama administration) represent only 11% of all return migrants to Mexico in that period. This means that a significant number of return migrants "chose" to go back to Mexico voluntarily.

Among its main findings, the study shows[2] that "Economic factors such as the U.S. recession and political factors such as immigration policy in both countries certainly have an impact on return migration patterns." The study also observed that "many [return migrants] are drawn emotionally to return to Mexico after 1–5 years, and most enjoy slightly higher incomes in Mexico upon their return than what they were earning in Mexico prior to migration." Notably, the study found that a large portion of these return migrants show a strong desire to remain in Mexico.

Economic Conditions Play a Key Role in Migration

These findings confirm some important claims. First, the economic conditions in both Mexico and the United States are key determinants in people's migration. As we have previously documented,[4] during the last few decades the changes in unauthorized migration have to a great extent followed the fluctuations in the U.S. economy. At the same time, improved economic conditions in Mexico,[5] as well as a sweeping reform of Mexico's immigration law[2] in 2011, have also impacted the reversal in the net migration flow between Mexico and the United States. However, this does not imply that this trend is irreversible. In fact, according to a recent [2013] report[6] by the Pew Research Center, the shrinking number of unauthorized migration to the United States recorded during and immediately after the Great Recession may be slightly on the rise in light of the improving U.S. economy. But the economic aspect, as important as it is, does not account for the whole story. There are also emotional factors that bond people to places. This applies both to migrants who feel their home is in Mexico and to those who are more attached to the United States. For example, among the migrants interviewed for the MATT study, over two-thirds of the migrants from Mexico to the United States had only intended to stay in the United States temporarily. The bottom line is that migrants tend to come to the United States when there is a demand for labor, and when economic opportunities are insufficient in Mexico. For the majority of Mexicans, however, migration would probably not be their first choice.

For many decades now, studies of international migration have uncovered structural factors that spur people to migrate from country to country, but the widespread view that migration is exclusively based on individuals' cost-benefit calculations continues to persist. According to this simplistic interpretation, people migrate because they are guided by their own economic interests. The problem with this type of interpretation is that it neglects some of the deeper causes that lead to migration.

International Migration Is a Complex Issue

As immigration expert Douglas Massey asserts,[7] a holistic understanding of international migration must at least account for (1) the structural forces that promote emigration from developing countries; (2) the structural forces that attract immigrants into developed nations; (3) the motivations, goals, and aspirations of people who respond to these structural forces; and (4) the social and economic structures that arise to connect areas of out and in-migrations.

Massey's understanding has enormous implications for immigration policy. If policy interventions aspire to be effective and realistic, they must rely on an in-depth comprehension of the issue. Unfortunately, this has not always been the case. For example, many efforts to curb illegal immigration into the U.S. have ignored the complex nature of international migration and, therefore, have failed[8] to meet their proposed goals. Specifically, policies that intend to tackle the problem of unauthorized migration through enforcement-only measures have proven to be not only very costly, but also ineffective. This is often largely the result of viewing undocumented immigrants as individu-

Reasons for Returning to Mexico

Main reasons cited for returning to Mexico from the United States:

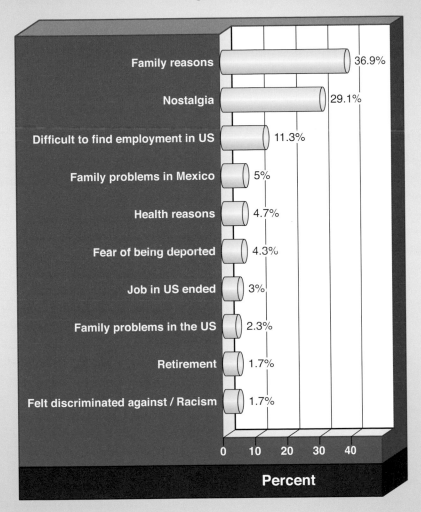

Reason	Percent
Family reasons	36.9%
Nostalgia	29.1%
Difficult to find employment in US	11.3%
Family problems in Mexico	5%
Health reasons	4.7%
Fear of being deported	4.3%
Job in US ended	3%
Family problems in the US	2.3%
Retirement	1.7%
Felt discriminated against / Racism	1.7%

Percent

Taken from: "The US/Mexico Cycle: The End of an Era: Quantitative Research Study Preliminary Findings and Insights," MATT.org, December 2013. www.matt.org.

als who choose to break the law without any reference to the larger context that allows for these activities to occur.

For policy makers in the United States, the findings of the MATT study[2] should ratify the need to create a new system for legal immigration that (1) is flexible enough to adjust to the fluctuations of the business cycle; (2) creates stronger channels for legal immigration when the economy is growing; (3) addresses the country's need for immigrants at all skill levels, and not just high-skilled workers; (4) provides mechanisms for border and immigration enforcement as part of a much larger and more comprehensive policy solution; (5) recognizes the fact that not all immigrants desire to migrate to the U.S. on a permanent basis; and (6) allows temporary immigrants to have a realistic pathway to become permanent residents if they wish to do so. In addition, the United States must find creative ways to cooperate with Mexico to ensure that economic prosperity in Mexico is a reality. If U.S. lawmakers do not tackle all these aspects in a comprehensive way, illegal immigration will likely become a permanent structural feature of the system.

Notes

1. www.wilsoncenter.org/event/mexican-immigrants-returning-to -mexico.
2. www.matt.org/uploads/2/4/9/3/24932918/returnmigration _top_line_www.pdf.
3. http://immigrationimpact.com/2013/12/20/new-ice-deporta tion-statistics-are-no-cause-for-celebration.
4. www.immigrationpolicy.org/just-facts/built-last-how-immigra tion-reform-can-deter-unauthorized-immigration.
5. www.pewhispanic.org/2012/04/23/net-migration-from-mexico -falls-to-zero-and-perhaps-less.
6. http://immigrationimpact.com/2013/09/24/possible-increase -in-unauthorized-immigration-brought-to-you-by-an-improv ing-economy.
7. www.russellsage.org/publications/handbook-international -migration.
8. www.immigrationpolicy.org/just-facts/fallacy-enforcement-first.

Mexico Should Take a More Active Stance on US Immigration Reform

Luis Rubio

"Mexico should be willing to commit to a broad migratory arrangement whereby it would control the flows of future potential migrants."

In the following viewpoint, Luis Rubio argues that Mexico can no longer afford to take a passive attitude on US immigration reform. This issue greatly affects Mexico, the author maintains, and the nation should find a way to be a partner in the solution. As Mexico sets the foundation for economic growth, Rubio contends that it must factor immigration policy into its future. He argues that Mexico should commit to a policy that reduces immigration to the United States. Rubio is chairman of the Center of Research for Development, a think tank in Mexico City, and the author of more than forty books on Mexican politics and economics. He also writes a weekly column for Mexico's *Reforma* newspaper.

1. The author claims that what percentage of Mexicans live outside the country?
2. If Mexico's economy continues to improve, what does Rubio predict will happen?
3. According to the author, what would result if Mexico commits to stemming immigration flows to the United States?

The Mexican government cannot afford the luxury of ignoring what is happening on immigration reform in the big and powerful North. And yet, it has taken a passive attitude. There are good historical reasons for this, but not a good one today.

Within the Mexican government as well as in Mexican society at large there are two clearly differentiated positions vis-à-vis the immigration debate in the United States. Some people consider the migratory theme an internal matter of the US and some consider it a matter of national interest for Mexico. The former would prefer to put on blinders; the latter would embark upon a crusade. Each has relevant arguments to support their claim.

Those who would rather stay aloof believe that immigration is a domestic issue because it involves what is most essential to any nation: the composition of its society. A sovereign government has the authority to decide on the legal treatment of people that may have violated its laws at the very instant of entering the country or when overstaying the time permitted on an entry stamp. Those taking this position do not want to tell the US what to do because they don't want the US to tell Mexico what it should do on this or other hot topics.

FAST FACT

According to the Migration Policy Institute, the leading countries of nationality of those apprehended at the US-Mexico border in 2010 were Mexico, Guatemala, El Salvador, and Honduras.

Then there are those who see the other side of the coin. More than 10 percent of the country's population lives outside of Mexico, the vast majority of them (97 percent) in the US. This constituency is

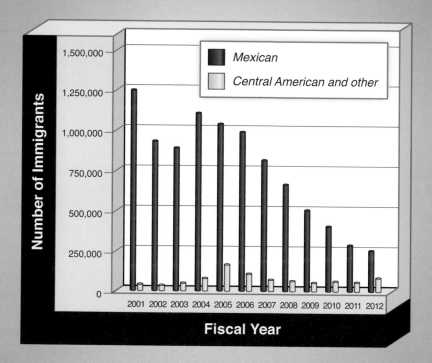

Nationality of Immigrants Crossing from Mexico to the United States

Number of Immigrants

1,500,000

1,250,000

1,000,000

750,000

500,000

250,000

0

■ Mexican

☐ Central American and other

2001 2002 2003 2004 2005 2006 2007 2008 2009 2010 2011 2012

Fiscal Year

Note: Federal fiscal years. 2012 projected. Data from Department of Homeland Security.

Taken from: Sebastian Rotella, "The New Border: Illegal Immigration's Shifting Frontier," ProPublica, December 6, 2012. www.propublica.org.

directly linked with a large part of the population (siblings, parents, children) back in Mexico. In some Mexican states, those connections represent more than half of the total number of its inhabitants. The government cannot ignore the obvious. Whatever decision the US ends up making on immigration, Mexico and Mexicans will be greatly affected. Hence, as much as the government might wish to lie low, this debate concerns vital matters that cannot be skirted.

As a result, Mexico's government seems to be straddling both views. On the one hand, the government is preparing Mexican consulates (a network of 51 offices directly linked to Mexican communities in the US, including Puerto Rico) to inform those potentially affected of

Mexican migrant farm workers harvest spinach in Colorado. Some immigration experts say that unauthorized immigrants will continue to come to the United States from Mexico and other countries as long as there is high demand for low-skilled workers.

the possible legal changes—and of their rights. Second, it is actively stating its position and preferences and, most likely, proposals that would help control future flows of workers in exchange for a broad liberalization for those already in the US. Finally, it is preparing to work with communities that are most affected by migrants in order to allay fears and advance its own perspective on the matter.

A decade ago, Mexico's government went out on a limb trying to advance legalization of those Mexicans working without papers in the US. Although there are disputes as to how advanced that process was, the fact is that September 11, 2001 ended all discussions and the then-Mexican president, Vicente Fox, was left with nothing to show for his efforts.

The current government wants neither to bet its success on decisions made in another country, nor to exert undue influence on the political process of a sovereign nation. In between these two positions, it is attempting to find a way to be a partner in the solution of a problem rather than the cause of one.

Mexico's government needs to make the case that migrants move North because there is demand for their labor there. Since there is no welfare or unemployment support for this cohort, people go when there are opportunities. There have been no work opportunities in the last few years and, therefore, potential migrants have stayed home. If Mexico's economy continues to improve, there will come a time when no Mexicans will move North. By the same token, as long as there is demand for low-skilled workers, they will continue flowing from Mexico or other nations. For the immigration reform to be successful, this reality needs to be incorporated into the new law.

As the Mexican economy attempts to create the foundations for a strong economic-growth era, the interest of the Mexican government is for Mexicans already in the US to secure a decent life. If that is secured as part of the US immigration-reform process, Mexico should be willing to commit to a broad migratory arrangement whereby it would control the flows of future potential migrants from or through Mexico's territory, whether they be Mexicans or other nationalities.

Mexico's government has never attempted to manage or hinder the flows of Mexican migrants to the US, considering that it is the constitutional right of any citizen to move about unimpeded. Committing to a change in this policy would entail a radical departure from Mexico's history as well as establish a transcendent legal precedent. The government would also be committing to stem flows not only from countries that are of concern to the US—Middle Eastern and the like, which it has controlled at least since 2001 (several Mexican immigration jails are full of migrants from all continents)—but also from Central American nations that do not constitute a security threat for the United States.

If Mexico commits to stemming immigration flows to the US, it could become a major source of stability for the immigration policy that the US decides to adopt. In fact, it could help the US establish a more rational and realistic mechanism to regulate migratory flows, just as other nations, such as Canada and Australia, do.

EVALUATING THE AUTHOR'S ARGUMENTS

In this viewpoint, Luis Rubio maintains that Mexico should play a more active role in US immigration reform. Why might someone argue that Mexico should not be more assertive regarding US immigration policy?

Chapter 3

How Should Mexico Approach the Drug War?

A member of the Mexican National Gendarmerie patrols in the tourist town of Valle de Bravo in Mexico state. The gendarmerie is a special unit of the federal police created as part of the Mexico's strategy to combat drug cartel crime.

Viewpoint

1

Mexico Can Win the Drug War

Jaime Daremblum

"Despite the terrible violence, the government is indeed winning [the drug war]."

In the following viewpoint, Jaime Daremblum argues that Mexico has the ability to win the drug war. Daremblum states that Mexico has seriously weakened most of the biggest drug cartels and established a cleaner, more effective federal police force. Although a high level of violence in the country persists, this does not mean the government's efforts have been ineffective, the author argues. Defeating the drug cartels will take time, Daremblum maintains, but ultimately, the Mexican government is winning the war. Daremblum is director of the Center for Latin American Studies at the Hudson Institute.

AS YOU READ, CONSIDER THE FOLLOWING QUESTIONS:

1. According to the author, organized-crime killings declined by what percentage between December 2012 and May 2013?
2. Where have the most substantial police reforms and aggressive criminal justice reforms taken place, according to Daremblum?
3. According to the author, what percentage of Mexicans still support using the army to battle the cartels?

I t often seems that every landmark victory in Mexico's war against organized crime is followed by a demoralizing or embarrassing setback. In December 2009, for example, Mexican naval forces killed Arturo Beltrán Leyva, one of the country's most notorious drug kingpins, after a two-hour firefight that also claimed the life of a courageous marine named Melquisedet Angulo, who was subsequently honored as a national hero.

Less than a week later, vengeful cartel gunmen brutally murdered Angulo's mother, his aunt and two of his siblings. More recently, in October 2012, the navy killed Heriberto Lazcano, boss of the spectacularly violent Zetas cartel. But then Lazcano's corpse was stolen from a funeral home by armed intruders. On July 15 [2013], the navy captured Lazcano's successor, Miguel Ángel Treviño, the most vicious drug lord in Mexico, without firing a shot. Unfortunately, the arrest of Treviño was quickly overshadowed by a surge of violence in the western state of Michoacán, including the July 28 [2013] killing of Vice Admiral Carlos Miguel Salazar, a senior naval official.

According to the Associated Press, the deadly attack on Salazar's SUV was apparently "the result of a series of tragic coincidences rather

Mario Cárdenas Guillén, the alleged leader of the Gulf drug cartel, is escorted in court by members of the Mexican navy in September 2012.

than a planned, targeted assassination." It was carried out by members of the Knights Templar cartel, an organization formed in 2011 after the destruction of a previous Michoacán-based cartel known as La Familia. In recent weeks [August 2013], Knights Templar gunmen have killed several police officers, and on July 22 they slaughtered five peaceful demonstrators in the town of Los Reyes. The gang has also orchestrated street protests against government security forces. When Salazar's car ran into a traffic jam caused by such a protest, the vice admiral decided to search for a different route back to his naval station. This led him down a rural side road, where he was ambushed.

Mexico's Drug War Is Complicated

Following the Treviño arrest, many foreign observers might have been tempted to say that Mexico was winning the cartel war. Following the murder of Vice Admiral Salazar and the related bloodshed in Michoacán, it is tempting to say that Mexico is losing the war. The truth is more complicated.

In a recent [July 25, 2013] Bloomberg piece, former Mexican intelligence officer Alejandro Hope offered what is probably the most accurate summary of where things stand: "While Mexico's fight against crime is moving in the right direction, it is doing so at a haltingly slow pace, much as it was a year ago."

The biggest problem, obviously, is the persistently high level of violence, although there is evidence that Mexico has made progress in reducing drug-related killings. A University of San Diego study found that, depending on which data source we consult, murders linked to organized crime either plateaued or fell significantly last year [2012]. For that matter, the Mexican government has reported that organized-crime killings declined by 18 percent between December 2012 and May 2013, compared with the prior six months. Yet researchers at the nonprofit Mexican Institute

> ## FAST FACT
>
> According to the *Washington Post*, when President Enrique Peña Nieto took office in 2012, he proposed the creation of five regional intelligence fusion centers and a ten-thousand-member super police force.

of Competitiveness estimate that the seasonally adjusted decline in all Mexican homicides between December and May was only 6 percent. That is still progress, of course, but the plain fact is that Mexico has a much higher murder rate today than it did when President Felipe Calderón deployed the military against the cartels back in December 2006. The violence is especially bad in Michoacán, in the neighboring state of Guerrero and in the border state of Coahuila.

Violence also remains high in the border state of Chihuahua. However, the state's largest city, Juárez, a onetime global murder capital, has witnessed a precipitous drop in drug-related violence. To be sure, the security gains in Juárez are partly—perhaps even largely—the result of one criminal organization (the Sinaloa cartel) either defeating or reaching a tentative truce with another (the Juárez cartel) in their battle for territorial control. But the city has also benefited from police reforms and social programs, including various initiatives undertaken by Chihuahua Governor César Duarte.

Judicial Reform Is Moving Slowly

For most of Mexico, state and local police reform is moving at a snail's pace. The same can be said of judicial reform, despite the major constitutional changes that were enacted in 2008. The most substantial police reforms have come in the state of Nuevo León (northeastern Mexico), while the most aggressive criminal justice reforms have taken place in Chihuahua, the state of Mexico (which surrounds Mexico City), and Morelos (which borders both Mexico state and Mexico City). There have also been significant judicial reforms in the states of Oaxaca (southwestern Mexico) and Zacatecas (north-central Mexico).

Mexican President Enrique Peña Nieto, who took office in December, has pledged to make judicial reform a top priority. As for the rest of his security agenda, Peña Nieto has indicated that he will reduce U.S. access to Mexican territory and Mexican intelligence, thereby reversing some of Calderón's policies. In general, he has downplayed talk of the drug war and drawn attention to Mexico's economic strengths.

And yet, the Treviño operation confirmed that U.S.-Mexico security cooperation will likely remain robust. According to Mexican-American scholar Ricardo Ainslie, author of "The Fight to Save Juárez," the Zeta

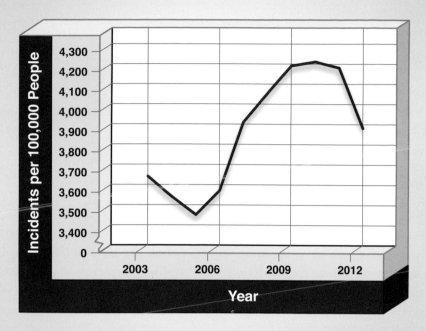

Violent Crime in Mexico

Incidents per 100,000 People

4,300
4,200
4,100
4,000
3,900
3,800
3,700
3,600
3,500
3,400
0

2003   2006   2009   2012

Year

Taken from: "Mexico Peace Index 2013," Institute for Economics and Peace, 2013, p. 22. http://economicsand peace.org.

leader was "tracked in real time by a U.S. Immigration and Customs Enforcement drone, while American intelligence monitored his communications and shared what was learned with Mexican authorities." Meanwhile, as InSight Crime analyst Patrick Corcoran has noted, the Mexican marines who arrested the Zeta leader were following his car in a U.S.-supplied Black Hawk helicopter.

With the capture of Treviño, 26 of the 37 drug lords identified by the Mexican government in March 2009 are now either dead or in prison. Twenty-five of those kingpins were taken out under President Calderón, who has been unjustly vilified for adopting policies that were necessary to establish the rule of law.

Indeed, when Calderón assumed the presidency in December 2006, five massively powerful cartels were threatening to turn Mexico into a narco-state. The country was already in the midst of an historic security crisis, with drug-related murders shooting up by nearly nine percent in 2005 and by nearly eleven percent in 2006, according to Harvard's Viridiana Ríos. News reports in December 2006 spoke of "escalating violence between warring drug cartels" (Associated Press) and said that certain regions of Mexico were "virtually paralyzed with tension" (*Los Angeles Times*), with border cities becoming "war zones" (*San Antonio Express-News*). Given the pervasive corruption at all levels of Mexican policing, Calderón had no choice but to unleash the military while simultaneously building a new and improved federal police force.

Mexico Is Winning the Drug War

Over the past seven years, all five of Mexico's largest 2006-era cartels have splintered, and one of them (La Familia) has been destroyed entirely. The Gulf, Juárez, and Tijuana cartels are all much less powerful and much more divided than they were a decade ago. The Zetas, who were part of the Gulf cartel until splitting off in 2010, remain Mexico's most violent criminal gang, but the government has now captured or killed four of the five most-wanted Zeta leaders it identified in 2009. The organization began fracturing last year, and the arrest of Treviño will further damage its internal cohesion. The Sinaloa cartel is still the country's biggest criminal enterprise, but its most lethal offshoot, the Beltrán Leyva cartel, was dismantled in 2010.

Not only has Mexico destroyed or seriously weakened most of the biggest cartels, it has also established a cleaner, more effective federal police force, while greatly improving its intelligence capabilities. The downside is that, by destabilizing and rupturing the cartels, Mexican authorities have created a more volatile and competitive criminal environment with higher levels of violence. Whereas the drug trade was once dominated by a handful of giant organizations, Mexican Attorney General Jesús Murillo believes there are now dozens of small or medium-sized trafficking groups. Unlike the larger, older cartels, these newer drug gangs cannot threaten the state itself, but they can generate enormous amounts of bloodshed.

Mexican police forces are not yet capable of handling the violence themselves; they still need military assistance. For all the criticism of Calderón's strategy, it's worth noting that, according to a March 2013 Pew Research Center survey, 85 percent of Mexicans still support using the army to battle the cartels. There is certainly a danger in becoming too reliant on the military, and Peña Nieto must not neglect the federal police. He must also do more than Calderón did to accelerate police and judicial reforms at the state and local levels. But as recent events have shown, the military remains an essential tool in Mexico's struggle against organized crime.

Given all that, is the Mexican government winning or losing the cartel war? Despite the terrible violence, the government is indeed winning. But transforming Mexico into a rule-of-law society will take many years. Anyone expecting rapid progress is likely to be disappointed.

EVALUATING THE AUTHOR'S ARGUMENTS

In this viewpoint, Jaime Daremblum claims that Mexico is winning the war against drugs. Based on what you have read, do you agree? Why or why not?

Mexico Cannot Win the Drug War

José Merino

"Can Mexico win the war against drugs? No."

In the following viewpoint, José Merino argues that Mexico has already lost the war against drugs. He highlights the national rate of homicides and the rise in small drug cartels. While these problems are not insurmountable, the author believes that Mexico's government does not have the ability to implement effective long-term drug-war strategies. Merino blames Mexico's corrupt and dysfunctional criminal justice system for the nation's defeat in the war against drugs. When the rule of law is not respected, he says, no war against criminals can be won. Merino is a professor of political science at the Instituto Tecnológico Autónomo de México in Mexico City.

AS YOU READ, CONSIDER THE FOLLOWING QUESTIONS:

1. What does winning the drug war mean, according to the author?
2. According to Merino, the national rate of homicides in Mexico rose by how much between 2007 and 2009?
3. The author claims that Mexico received what score in effective criminal justice on the World Justice Project Rule of Law Index 2011?

Can Mexico win the war against drugs? No. If winning means eliminating all drug production, trade and consumption, then the only honest answer is "no." The strategic lines drawn by the Mexican government rely on "containment and weakening" criminal organizations, not "elimination." Even if we assume a sharp reduction in the consumption of drugs in the United States, significant demand will remain, and supply will most probably come from south of the border. Of course, given the scale of this illegal trade, relatively large and well-organized groups will be required to meet demand.

What can "winning the war" possibly mean, then? It means the reduction of the main negative side effects of the trade: violence and the weakening of the rule of law.

Examining the Crime Statistics

Unfortunately, the indicators of violence in Mexico force us to conclude that we have painfully lost.

The national rate of homicides (per 100,000 inhabitants) moved from 8.4 in 2007 to 18.0 in 2009 (according to the National Institute of Statistics, Geography and Informatics, INEGI) or from 9.7 in 2007 to 15.0 in 2009 (according to the National System for National Security, SNSP). But in the eight states in which federal and local forces ran joint operations against criminal organizations, the 2007–2009 changes went from 12.8 to 41.3 (INEGI data) or from 15.9 to 34.5 (SNSP) per 100,000. I recently estimated that, due to these joint operations, homicides in those states increased by 12,000 between 2007 and 2010 (*Nexos*, June 2011). Eighty-five municipalities account for 70 percent of total homicides in Mexico, but the increase has been broader: the number of Mexicans living in a municipality with homicide rates above 50 per 100,000 people moved from 850,000 in 2007 to 9.1 million in 2009.

For the last five years, Mexicans have become experts at body counts, but we still are unable to understand the causes of those deaths. Worse, we have become accustomed to seeing bodies, where we ought to be seeing lawful prosecutions.

This leads to the second side effect. Experts and some government officials argue that the main goal of the strategy started in 2007 was to dismantle big cartels and fragment them into smaller cells so that

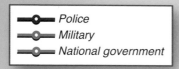

Mexicans' Confidence in Local Police, Military, and National Government

Percentage of Mexico residents who say they have confidence in . . .

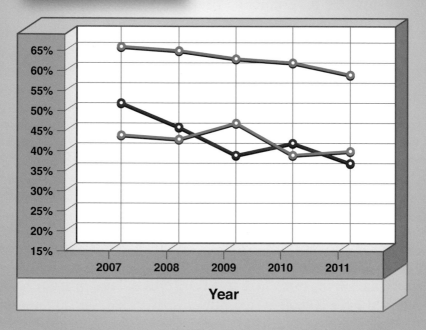

— Police
— Military
— National government

Taken from: Peter Cynkar, "Opinion Briefing: Mexico's Drug War," Gallup, April 4, 2012. www.gallup.com.

they would not represent a serious threat. That is, to turn a national security menace into a public security problem.

According to a study presented by Mexican security analyst Eduardo Guerrero (*Nexos*, June 2011) the number of cartels in Mexico climbed from six to 12 between 2007 and 2010, while the number of smaller local organizations increased from five to 62 in the same period. Intuitively, smaller organizations face higher restrictions for trafficking large amounts of drugs across the border, and consequently are forced to expand their operations to other illegal activities: Mexico's rate of extortion increased from 3.0 (per 100,000 inhabitants) in 2007 to 5.5 in 2010. Kidnappings went from 0.4 to 1.2 (per 100,000 inhabitants).

The Rise of Small Drug Cartels Is a Serious Problem

We are trapped in a worst-case scenario: giant cartels such as Sinaloa continue to be a threat and new, violent small cells are being created and expanding the range of their criminal activities.

Achieving the government's goal of transforming the national problem into a series of local ones depends on the quality of local police—and that is another serious problem. By December 2010, in 29 of Mexico's 32 states, less than 50 percent of state police officers had been subjected to a Trust Test (*prueba de confianza*), which included polygraph and drug tests to identify cops who likely were or would become accomplices to criminals. Only two states have conducted such tests on more than 50 percent of their municipal police forces. Worse, as many as 65 percent of the state and municipal officers who took those tests failed them, leading national authorities to conclude that they may be linked to criminal organizations.

> **FAST FACT**
>
> The Congressional Research Service finds that Mexican drug trafficking organizations engage in a wide variety of criminal activities in addition to selling drugs, including kidnapping, assassination for hire, auto theft, prostitution, extortion, money laundering, and human smuggling.

No one would argue that the Mexican government should turn its attention away from the drug cartels. However, since the inception of the current strategy, the government has never allowed citizens the legal tools to fight this battle. Mexicans do not find their government a dependable ally against criminals. And Mexico's judicial system remains embarrassingly corrupt, biased and inept.

The increase in lethal violence has not been accompanied by a corresponding increase in prosecutions. On the contrary, we have seen the systematic "presentation" of unconvicted suspects before the news

Relatives mourn at a 2014 funeral in Michoacán State, Mexico, of a man killed by soldiers who had been deployed to the region to disarm civilians who were fighting a drug cartel. In recent years, the homicide rate in Mexico has increased as the number of smaller drug cartels has grown.

media, and continued abuses by authorities that result in no legal consequences. The killing of two boys in Tamaulipas in April 2010 and the manipulation of a crime scene where two graduate students were killed at *Tecnológico de Monterrey* in March 2010 are just two recent prominent cases documented by the National Commission on Human Rights.

These concerns help explain why Mexico received a score of 0.3 (out of 1) in "effective criminal justice" on the World Justice Project Rule of Law Index 2011, placing 63rd in a list of 66 countries evaluated. We had the worst performance in Latin America in terms of corruption, law enforcement and access to civil justice.

There have been efforts to change. However, a bill approved by Congress in 2008, changing the Mexican judicial system to an adversarial model with oral trials to make it more expeditious and fair, hasn't even been implemented yet.

Mexico Has Lost the Drug War

How can we possibly fight a war against drugs when we have such an inefficient and dysfunctional criminal justice system? How can Mexican citizens trust authorities when we are denied legal certainty, due process and access to justice—especially when we routinely see proof of complicity between criminals and police?

No war against criminals can be won where the rule of law is not respected, defended and deepened.

Government officials frequently remind us that an effective strategy to counter crime should result from social policies promoting education, health and income opportunities. I could not agree more. Perhaps the most important government action to prevent a young Mexican from participating in criminal activities is to allow him or her to foresee a productive future within the limits of the law. We must be doing something wrong when a Mexican teen chooses a short criminal life instead of a long life on the right side of the law.

Winning the fight against drugs requires an aggressive use of financial intelligence to combat money laundering, as well as a clear diplomatic effort to question the current punitive model and explore decriminalization schemes. However, two key tools any society needs to fight organized crime—respect for the rule of law and the creation of opportunities for young people to earn legitimate income—have been undermined in Mexico. We've become the living, wounded proof of the limits of a battle based primarily on the use of force. And we've lost.

EVALUATING THE AUTHOR'S ARGUMENTS

In this viewpoint, José Merino argues that Mexico's criminal justice system does not have the ability to win the war against drugs. Whose argument is more convincing, the author's or that of Jaime Daremblum, the author of the preceding viewpoint? Why?

US Weapons Fuel the Mexican Drug War

Chris McGreal

"The [Mexican drug] cartel is armed by weapons from American gun shops."

In the following viewpoint, Chris McGreal argues that Mexico's drug cartels are supported by the US weapons industry. He maintains that US gun laws encourage trafficking because traffickers are able to access a high volume of weapons for a low cost. Many members of law enforcement support making weapons trafficking a federal crime. However, the author contends that any weapons-trafficking legislation faces strong resistance from the powerful gun lobby that opposes tightening gun laws. McGreal is the Washington correspondent for the British newspaper *The Guardian* and a former BBC journalist in Central America.

AS YOU READ, CONSIDER THE FOLLOWING QUESTIONS:

1. According to the author, the drug war in Mexico has claimed how many lives in five years?
2. How many US states require identification to purchase ammunition, as stated by McGreal?
3. According to the author, how many firearms seized by Mexico over the previous five years were traced to the United States?

If anyone at Academy sports shop in Houston was suspicious as John Hernandez pushed $2,600 in cash across the counter, they kept it to themselves.

The 25 year-old unemployed machinist in dark glasses walked out of the gun shop clutching three powerful assault rifles modelled on the US army's M-16.

A few weeks later, Hernandez bought five similar weapons at another Houston gun shop, Carter's Country. There were few questions on that occasion, either, or as he visited other weapons stores across the city in the following months until he had bought a total of 14 assault rifles and nine other weapons for nearly $25,000.

With each purchase, all the law required was that Hernandez prove he lived in Texas and wait a few minutes while the store checked he had no criminal record.

Months later, one of those assault rifles was seized in neighbouring Mexico at the scene of the "Acapulco police massacre", after one of the country's most powerful drug cartels killed five officers and two secretaries in an attack at the beach resort once regarded as a millionaires' playground. Another was recovered after the kidnap and murder of a cattle buyer. Others were found in the hands of top-level enforcers for narcotics traffickers, or abandoned after attacks on Mexican police and the military. The guns have been tied to eight killings in Mexico.

In time, US federal agents discovered that Hernandez was at the heart of a ring of two dozen people who bought more than 300 weapons from Texas gun shops for one of the more notorious Mexican drug cartels, Los Zetas. Some of those guns have since been linked to the killings of at least 18 Mexican police officers and civilians, including members of the judiciary and a businessman who was abducted and murdered.

US Law Encourages Gun Trafficking

The weapons bought by Hernandez and his ring were just a fraction of the tens of thousands smuggled across the US's southern border to cartels fighting a bloody war with the Mexican government that has claimed about 45,000 lives in five years.

It's a war sustained by a merry-go-round. The cartels use the money paid by Americans for drugs to buy weapons at US guns stores, which are then shipped across the frontier, often using the same vehicles and routes used to smuggle more narcotics north. The weapons are used by the cartels to protect narcotics production in their battle with the Mexican police and army, and smuggle drugs north.

Key to the cycle is the ease with which traffickers are able to obtain guns in the US, made possible in large part by the robust opposition of the powerful gun lobby—backed by much of the US Congress—to tighter laws against arms trafficking.

"The United States is the easiest and the cheapest place for drug traffickers to get their firearms, and as long as we are the easiest and cheapest place for the cartels to get their firearms there'll continue to be gun trafficking," said J Dewey Webb, the special agent in charge of pursuing weapons traffickers in Texas at the US Bureau of Alcohol, Tobacco, Firearms and Explosives (ATF).

Kristen Rand, director of the Violence Policy Centre which campaigns for greater gun control, said drug traffickers face little more than a few logistical difficulties in buying weapons in America.

"If you wanted to design a set of laws to encourage gun trafficking, that is what the US has done," she said. "The traffickers are able to access a high volume of assault weapons, sniper rifles, armour-piercing handguns. All the weapons they need to wage war are readily available on the civilian market. There's basically nothing to stop them other than the annoyance of having to round up enough people to buy them.". . .

It's even easier to buy ammunition. While many US states demand a driving licence to buy common types of cold medicine that can also be used to manufacture the drug meth amphetamine, not a single state requires identification to purchase ammunition, even in large quantities.

The United States Arms Mexican Drug Cartels

According to the US Government Accountability Office, 87% of firearms seized by Mexico over the previous five years were traced to the US. Texas was the single largest source. The US attorney general, Eric Holder, told Congress last month [November 2011] that of 94,000 weapons captured from drug traffickers by the Mexican authorities, over 64,000 originated in the US.

One of the most senior members of the Zetas, Jesus Enrique Rejon Aguilar, said after his capture in July that the cartel is armed by weapons from American gun shops.

"All the weapons are bought in the United States," he said in a video recorded by the Mexican federal police.

Only legal residents of Texas can buy guns over the counter, so the cartels use people such as Hernandez, who has since been jailed for eight years along with other members of his ring, as "straw purchasers".

"We see them being paid $50 to $500 a time. In these times, that's a lot of money for folks," said Webb. "What we've seen with the cartels is very elaborate schemes. They have people that handle the money. They have people that handle the transportation of the weapons. They use the same infrastructure they use to bring the drugs in. Sometimes even the same vehicles that move the narcotics north are the vehicles that move the firearms and the ammunition and money south."

FAST FACT

The *New York Times* reports that Mexico has only one legal gun store; in comparison, there are 49,762 licensed gun dealers in the United States.

The straw buyers are mostly in search of guns such as AK-47s and Armalite assault rifles, which were popular with the IRA [Irish Republican Army], as well as powerful pistols such as the Belgian-made FN. All are available over the counter in thousands of gun shops. . . .

Weapons Trafficking Legislation Faces Resistance

In July [2011], two Democratic party members of Congress sponsored legislation to make weapons trafficking a federal crime. It has widespread support among police officers including the Federal Law Enforcement Officers Association which represents more than 26,000 federal agents. . . .

But the bill is facing stiff resistance from a gun lobby that says new laws are the thin end of a wedge that will result in the government confiscating all weapons. Wayne LaPierre, chief executive of the

Semiautomatic weapons are on display at a gun shop in Texas near the Mexican border. Straw purchasers buy firearms legally in US border states, and the weapons are then transported illegally into Mexico for use by drug cartels.

National Rifle Association [NRA], one of the most powerful lobby groups in the US, has said that tightening gun laws will penalise hunters and those Americans who buy firearms for self-defence.

Many members of Congress, often with one eye on the NRA, are also resistant.

Politicians who speak alarmingly of the threat to the US from the bloodshed on its southern border, and use it to call for tighter immigration controls, are often the ones who most strongly oppose even the most minimal new measures to stem the flow of weapons.

A report by the US senate's narcotics control caucus in June said: "Congress has been virtually moribund while powerful Mexican drug trafficking organisations continue to gain unfettered access to military-style firearms coming from the United States." . . .

The [Barack] Obama administration has spurned appeals to reinstate a ban on the importation of AK-47s and other kinds of foreign-made assault rifles that was in place during the Clinton administration but dropped by President [George W.] Bush.

The ATF, which falls under Holder's jurisdiction, earlier this year began requiring gun shops in the four US states bordering Mexico to report to authorities if the same person buys two or more assault rifles and some other guns over a five-day period. Congress has tried to block the measure, to Holder's frustration. . . .

Although restrained by his position from openly criticising the politics of the issue, [Webb] is clearly frustrated at the unwillingness of Congress to act.

"There's some common sense things about the way things should be done," he said.

But ultimately, Webb says it's the drug buyers who are responsible.

"Every person that pays for that marijuana, that meth, that cocaine is paying for the tools of the trade which are guns. Those people that are buying the drugs are just as responsible as the people buying those guns, just as responsible as the people pulling the triggers in Mexico. The drug use in this country is fuelling that machine. It's a never-ending cycle," he said.

Mexico's president sees it differently.

"Why does this arms business continue?" Calderon said in June. "I say it openly: it's because of the profit which the US arms industry makes."

EVALUATING THE AUTHOR'S ARGUMENTS

In this viewpoint, Chris McGreal claims that the US weapons industry supports Mexican drug cartels. On the basis of the author's argument, do you believe that enacting tighter gun laws in the United States would have an impact on the drug war in Mexico? Why or why not?

US Weapons Are Not to Blame for the Drug War

Ted Galen Carpenter

"The argument that supposedly lax U.S. gun laws are a major reason for Mexico's drug violence is a bit of a red herring."

In the following viewpoint, Ted Galen Carpenter argues that the US weapons industry is not responsible for drug-related gun violence in Mexico. While some believe that permissive gun laws in the United States support gun trafficking and contribute to Mexico's drug war, Carpenter believes this argument is flawed because the drug cartels access guns from a variety of sources—not just the United States. Winning Mexico's drug war, he says, requires drug legalization, not gun trafficking legislation. Carpenter believes reducing the profit from the drug trade is the only effective way to reduce crime in Mexico. Carpenter is a senior fellow at the Cato Institute, a contributing editor to the *National Interest*, and the author of numerous books on international affairs, including *The Fire Next Door: Mexico's Drug Violence and the Danger to America*.

AS YOU READ, CONSIDER THE FOLLOWING QUESTIONS:
1. According to the author, what is the underlying reason for Mexico's drug violence?
2. What is Mexico's share of the global illegal-drug trade, as stated by the author?
3. According to Carpenter, what percentage of the price of illegal drugs is the result of their illegality?

Mexico's illegal-drug trade and the accompanying violence there and in neighboring Central American countries is again a hot topic for members of the foreign-policy community in the United States. The latest catalyst is a new study [July 2013] from the Council on Foreign Relations [CFR] arguing that the "flow of high-powered weaponry from the United States exacerbates the soaring rates of gun-related violence in the region."

It is hardly a new argument. Former secretary of state Hillary Clinton repeatedly embraced the Mexican government's view that permissive gun laws in the United States were a major contributor to the drug-related violence that has now claimed an estimated eighty thousand in Mexico over the past six-and-a-half years. In summit meetings with both the current Mexican president and his predecessor, President [Barack] Obama has adopted a similar position. But such arguments misconstrue the symptoms of the problem for the cause. The underlying reason for Mexico's agony is not the easy availability of guns, but the enormous profitability of the illegal-drug trade and the various pathologies that it spawns, including violence and pervasive corruption.

Examining the CFR Study

The CFR study's author, Julia Sweig, Nelson and David Rockefeller Senior Fellow for Latin American Studies at the Council, is unsparing in her criticism of U.S. policy. With the launch of the 2007 Mérida Initiative to combat drug trafficking, Sweig contends, "the U.S. and Mexican governments agreed to a regional security framework guided by the principle of shared responsibility. Among its domestic obligations, the United States committed to intensify its efforts to combat the illegal trafficking of weapons and ammunition into Mexico." Six years later, she charges, "little has changed: the U.S. civilian firearms market continues to supply the region's transnational criminal networks with high-powered weaponry that is purchased with limited oversight."

In contrast, she praises Latin American governments for having "moved to disarm criminal networks by tightening their own gun law codes. Mexico prohibits the sale of handguns with calibers greater than .38," and Mexico, along with several other countries, "have implemented gun buyback programs." Given the drug-related carnage in Mexico and its Central American neighbors in recent years, it would appear that the strategy Sweig cites hasn't worked very well. To be blunt, the Sinaloa cartel, the Zetas, and other trafficking organizations are not going to be stopped, or even seriously inconvenienced, by tougher gun-control measures in the United States.

US Gun Laws Do Not Cause Mexican Violence

Indeed, the argument that supposedly lax U.S. gun laws are a major reason for Mexico's drug violence is a bit of a red herring. It's not

Members of the Mexican navy escort drug cartel members in January 2011; the hundreds of weapons on display were seized during the arrest. Some argue that drug cartels obtain weapons from many different sources, not just from US gun shops.

Illegal Drug Trade Rivals Mexico's Highest Value Exports

The value of illegal drug exports from Mexico is estimated to be US$30 billion—a figure that would place this underground economy among the top five export categories for the country in 2013.

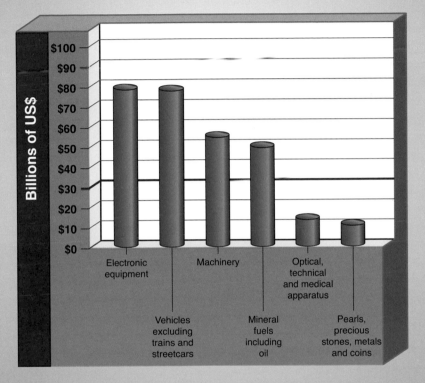

Note: Estimate of illegal drug exports taken from Brianna Lee, "Mexico's Drug War," Council on Foreign Relations Backgrounder, March 5, 2014.

Taken from: Daniel Workman, "Highest Value Mexican Export Products," World's Top Exports, April 19, 2014. www.worldstopexports.com.

to say that the cartels don't get some of their weaponry from gun shops, flea markets, pawn shops, and gun shows in the United States, as Sweig charges. They do, but they also get them from numerous other sources. As I note in chapter nine of my latest book [*The Fire Next Door: Mexico's Drug Violence and the Danger to America* (2012)] on the international drug war, the cartels obtain weapons from the international black market, the armories of Central American countries the U.S. helped fill during the fight against communist infiltration of the region in the 1980s, and even Mexico's own military depots.

The principal reason that the drug gangs can obtain all the firepower they want from multiple sources is that they have vast financial resources at their disposal. Mexico's share of the $300 billion to $350 billion global illegal-drug trade is estimated to be at least $35 billion, and according to the former DEA liaison at the U.S. embassy in Mexico City, perhaps as much as $60 billion, per year. That sum is in a country that the CIA estimates has a modest legal gross domestic product of $1.18 trillion. In other words, the drug trade is equal to at least 3 percent and perhaps nearly 6 percent of Mexico's entire economy.

That enormous wealth gives the cartels the power to corrupt, intimidate, or eliminate law-enforcement personnel, media figures, elected officials, and business leaders nearly at will. They even have the financial clout to tempt large, respected financial institutions in the United States and other countries into laundering their profits.

Restricting Gun Access Is Futile

As long as the traffickers possess such funds, trying to halt their turf fights over the valuable trafficking routes into the United States by restricting access to guns is as futile as the reputed attempt of King Canute to hold back the tides. A far more effective solution would be to greatly reduce the profits available from the drug trade. Nearly 90 percent of the retail price of illegal drugs is simply the result of their illegality. Ending the failed prohibition strategy, both domestically and internationally, would drastically slow the flow of profits. Mexico's former president Vicente Fox, Brazil's former president Fernando Henrique Cardoso, and a growing roster of past and present Latin American leaders seem to be reaching that conclusion. A Mexican drug industry of $4 billion or $5 billion a year would pose considerably less danger to Mexico's government and society than one nine or ten times that size. That's true even if the trade remained exclusively in the hands of criminal elements—which, absent prohibition, it probably would not.

It is time for a strategy that gets to the root cause of Mexico's drug-related corruption and violence, not merely attempts to treat the symptoms with the legislative equivalent of patent medicine. The only way to significantly reduce the violence is to defund the cartels. And that requires rethinking the entire prohibition strategy.

EVALUATING THE AUTHOR'S ARGUMENTS

In this viewpoint, Ted Galen Carpenter argues that drug legalization is a more effective way to end the drug war in Mexico than stricter gun legislation. Whose argument is more convincing, the author's or Chris McGreal's? Explain your answer.

Viewpoint 5

Stop the Drugs War

Mary Wakefield

In the following viewpoint, Mary Wakefield argues that the drug war in Mexico cannot be won by military action. Instead, she maintains that the only way to win the war is to legalize drugs. While this is a dramatic step, the author contends that the drug war's cost in human lives is too high. The best option, she says, is to win the war without fighting. By legalizing drugs, the author believes, the cartels would be demolished, the big profits would be in legitimate business, the crime rate would drop, and Mexico's tourism industry would get a boost. Wakefield is deputy editor of *The Spectator*, a British magazine.

> *"If fighting doesn't work, why not legalise drugs instead?"*

AS YOU READ, CONSIDER THE FOLLOWING QUESTIONS:

1. According to the author, what percentage of Mexican drug cartels are selling cannabis in the United States?
2. What would be the result of legalizing drugs in Mexico, according to Wakefield?
3. As stated by the author, how has the drug war in Mexico impacted tourism?

'They're all bad, our politicians, all corrupt,' said Maria, her cheery face dissolving into distaste. What about the new president, Peña Nieto? I ask. 'That pretty boy? Ugh!'

It was late afternoon in Oaxaca's central square, the Zocolo. Clouds were cruising in from the Sierra Madre and the dogs had begun to squabble and hump outside the cathedral. The news kiosk looked like a missing person's bureau, each front page full of mugshots: the latest victims of the drug wars.

Drug Policy Positions in Mexico and Central America

Open to debate on drug decriminalization and legalization

Has partial decriminalization laws or has argued in favor of decriminalization, but is against legalization

Against both decriminalization and legalization of drugs

MEXICO

BELIZE
HONDURAS
GUATEMALA
EL SALVADOR
NICARAGUA
COSTA RICA
PANAMA

Taken from: InSight Crime, "Country-by-Country Map of Drug Policy Positions in the Americas," July 25, 2013. www.insightcrime.org.

What about Calderon, the one before Peña Nieto, I asked Maria, who's seen ten presidents come and go. Wasn't he OK? At least he tried to fight the drug cartels. 'He's loco! Mad,' said Maria, with a dismissive shrug. 'His so-called drug war—pah! Do you know how many have died in the drug war? They say 50,000 dead but it's more like 100,000. It is more than died in the Vietnam War. And these are not soldiers, they are young boys, babies, mothers, husbands. And for what?'

There's the question: for what? Felipe Calderon was once convinced he had the answer: to crack down on the kingpins; restore moral order. But Calderon's war had a pretty clear outcome: the bad guys won. Capos were shot, but their cartels just split and proliferated: more gang warfare, more severed heads dumped on beaches; more corpses carved up and left on busy streets for kids to gawp at; extortion, kidnap, rape. It soon became clear even to Calderon that the 'war on drugs' was unwinnable, for the simple reason that the cause of the mayhem is not in Mexico, it's in the States. For as long as there are American junkies, Mexico will pay the blood price for their addiction.

This has been the status quo for the past few decades, and as far as I could tell on my Mexican adventure last year, Maria was right: no one expected Peña Nieto to change much of anything. He belongs to the PRI—the Institutional Revolutionary Party, which ruled Mexico for most of the past century, and its approach to the cartels has been a blind eye.

But late last year, there was a new twist: America, having spent billions on Calderon's daft crusade, last month voted to legalise cannabis in some states (if the federal government gives them the OK). Colorado and Washington started it, California is keen to follow suit, and Oregon, Rhode Island, Maine and Vermont aren't far behind. It creates an irony that the Mexican president is puzzling over: some 40 per cent of the cartels' business is selling cannabis across the border, so why should Mexico bust a gut keeping it from getting to America, if it's legal there? This new legislation, said one of Peña Nieto's advisers cautiously, 'changes the rules of the game'.

It does, and it also creates an opportunity, though one that Peña Nieto might not welcome. If the Mexican president is brave enough, he could not just follow the new rules, but perhaps change the game. He could follow the lead of President Otto Pérez Molina of Guatemala, who has asked the question: if fighting doesn't work, why not legalise drugs instead? Molina is a former head of the intelligence services who has himself tried the iron-fist approach to gangs, but now he says the price paid in human lives is too high. 'It's time to end the myths, the taboos, and discuss legalisation.'

Perhaps it sounds like a dramatic step. It's certainly one America would oppose with every star and stripe, because to legalise drugs in Mexico would be to push the fight alarmingly close to their border. But then, even as a tourist there, you can see Mexico requires a dramatic step.

To say that the police aren't effective is an almost comic understatement. It's not just that there are good cops and bad cops; it's that it's impossible to tell the difference. Take this little tangle. Last year, in June, there was a shootout in the food court of Mexico City airport, Terminal 2. Three police officers who suspected another three of drug-smuggling went (they say) to make an arrest. The drug-running cops opened fire, killed the good cops, then skipped off scot-free, leaving clumps of traumatised Texan tourists shivering under canteen tables, vowing never to leave Dallas again. It later turned out that the runaway cops were in fact the good guys. They had been about to expose all the other cops as drug-smugglers, and had been shot at as a result. All 348 airport cops were later re-shuffled to other states.

If you think perhaps the answer to Mexico's troubles is a tougher army, then I'd like to introduce you to Los Zetas. They are often also described as the paramilitary wing of the older Gulf Cartel, but that hasn't been true for a while. In 2010 they bit off the hand that fed them, formed their own gang, and began to show their rivals the true meaning of brutality. The Zetas specialise in the butchering of children. They have been phenomenally successful, just recently overtaking the famous Sinaloa cartel and dominating the country. How have they managed this? Because they came from the army, from Mexico's equivalent of the SAS. They

Vicente Fox (right), a former president of Mexico, speaks during the opening of the US-Mexico symposium on the legalization and medical use of marijuana. Some experts believe that legalizing drugs would end the drug wars.

were trained by American and Israeli special forces in intimidation, ambushing and marksmanship, just to fight the drug gangs. Then they upped and formed one. The Zetas still recruit from Mexico's special forces and from the Guatemalan equivalent, the Kaibiles. The more cash America puts into training the Mexican army, the happier the Zetas are, purring over all the potential new recruits.

So there aren't really many other alternatives. Why not legalise drugs? It wouldn't be giving up, it would be winning without fighting—the best, cleverest way. The cartels would be forced above ground; the big money would be in legitimate business . . . and who knows, the police might once again become an effective force.

After leaving Oaxaca, I headed for Veracruz state on the Mexican gulf and Maria waved us off with a warning: 'Be careful, Los Zetas operate there!' The next night was an anxious one, high in the Sierra Norte Mountains, Googling for signs of trouble. The whole police force had been sacked recently, it turned out, and the Zetas were waging a war against journalists, leaving their beaten bodies in the streets as a warning to others. That was enough for me. At the turn-off to Veracruz the following day, we turned tail and made for safer-sounding Villahermosa, though I'm quite sure the chances of us actually meeting a Zeta were very slim.

And that's another tragedy for Mexico. It's a terrific place, but tourists are increasingly so paralysed with anxiety about the cartels that they're reluctant to travel there. We ate alone one night in a three-storey restaurant in Mexico City on the main square—the one the *Lonely Planet* said was usually chock-a-block. Waiters idled by the walls, waiting to go home. A hundred tables laid in high season, and only two customers all night. If tourism dries up, there'll be only one career for a young man with an eye to making money: join a gang.

President Peña Nieto is not a tough guy like Guatemala's Molina. He will need help steeling himself to even consider legalisation. But perhaps he should look for inspiration at the official logo of Los Zetas. Along with a shield and a gun, they've included the drawing of a puppet-master's hand, taken from the poster for Coppola's *Godfather* movies. It's two fingers up to the government: we really run the show. But it's also the clue to what could be their undoing. If they're up to speed with American gangster history, they'll know that it was only by ending prohibition that America did for Al Capone.

EVALUATING THE AUTHOR'S ARGUMENTS

In this viewpoint, Mary Wakefield contends that the only way to win the drug war in Mexico is to legalize drugs there. Do you agree with the author, or do you believe the drug war can be fought successfully with military action? Explain your answer.

US Support for Mexican Reforms Would Decrease Drug Violence

Shannon K. O'Neil

"U.S.-Mexico security cooperation ... is vital and must continue."

In the following viewpoint, Shannon K. O'Neil discusses the United States' security relationship with Mexico. The two countries are linked, she says, and a strong and safe Mexico will have positive benefits for the United States. The author argues that the United States should adjust its strategy by providing financial support for Mexican judicial reform, state and local security efforts, and the modernization of the US-Mexico border. These efforts would help Mexico lower its crime rate and benefit the economies of both countries, she maintains. O'Neil is senior fellow for Latin America Studies with the Council on Foreign Relations.

Given our deep economic, personal, and community ties, Mexico's safety and security is vital to [the United States]. A strong and safe Mexico will have positive benefits for the United States, while a dangerous Mexico will have repercussions far beyond the southern U.S. border.

Refocusing U.S.-Mexico Security Cooperation

U.S.-Mexico security cooperation, led by the Merida Initiative,[1] is vital and must continue. But Mexico's political landscape has changed under the Enrique Peña Nieto government, and the United States must adjust its strategy and support accordingly. Building on the lessons of the past five years, the United States should work with Mexico to implement the nonmilitary programs envisioned in the current Merida framework, in particular supporting and prioritizing Mexico's ongoing judicial reform, training police officers at the state and local levels, investing in local community and youth-oriented programs, and modernizing the U.S.-Mexico border. . . .

Changing Realities on the Ground

As the U.S.-Mexico security cooperation strategy has evolved, so too have the realities on the ground. The most drastic shift is the rise in violence. When the Merida Initiative was signed in 2007, there were just over two thousand drug-related homicides annually; by 2012, the number escalated to more than twelve thousand. Violence also spread from roughly 50 municipalities in 2007 (mostly along the border and in Sinaloa) to some 240 municipalities throughout Mexico in 2011, including the once-safe industrial center of Monterrey and cities such as Acapulco, Nuevo Laredo, and Torreon.

This increase in violence is not just the direct result of drug trafficking. Criminal organizations have diversified into numerous illicit businesses, including kidnapping, robbery, human trafficking, extortion, and retail drug sales, and as a result prey more directly on the local population. One recent survey found that over 40 percent of Mexicans reported that they or a family member had been a victim of a crime in the past year.

Mexico's politics have also changed. On December 1, 2012, Enrique Peña Nieto became president, bringing the Institutional Revolutionary Party's (PRI) back into Los Pinos, Mexico's White House. During his campaign, he promised to shift the country's current security strategy away from combating drug trafficking toward reducing violence. Throughout his first six months however he has been somewhat slow to define the details of his new security approach, though the general announcements reflect more continuity than change. Peña Nieto's National Development Plan maintains a role for the armed forces, and in fact calls for creating a firmer legal basis for the military's public security role. He has said he will continue to push through the judicial

Motorists wait in congested traffic to enter the United States from Mexico at the Tijuana-San Diego border in 2013. Some experts suggest that modernizing border crossings would improve security and business opportunities between the two countries.

reform begun in 2008. He has also promised to build on programs such as *Todos Somos Juárez*, expanding and prioritizing broad-based crime prevention efforts.

Some strategic changes are planned. The government has announced it will create a new national gendarmerie, a 40,000 member force. It has also begun the process of centralizing control and command of the security apparatus under the Ministry of the Interior, beginning with folding the autonomous Federal Police back under its wing. . . .

U.S.-Mexico Security Cooperation Going Forward

These announced changes will lead to some shifts in how U.S. law enforcement and other agencies work with Mexico on security issues. Within the United States there are worries that these changes will stifle cooperation, and in particular the flow of information—especially sensitive intelligence—that has been important in many of the successful operations and takedowns of recent years. But the most recent articulation by the Mexican government should not be seen as the last or permanent word on the future of U.S.-Mexico security cooperation. Instead, it should be considered as part of the ongoing discussion and evolution in the relationship that has happened, that is happening, and that will continue to happen in the coming months and years. . . .

U.S. assistance will undoubtedly remain a small portion of the overall security spending in Mexico, as it should be. But with the funds that the United States does dedicate, it should prioritize civilian (versus military) law enforcement institutions, and focus on four areas. The first is judicial reform, as long-term sustainable security will only exist when Mexico has a strong civilian-based rule of law, and is able to take on and punish all types of criminal activity.

> **FAST FACT**
>
> According to the *Washington Post*, in the late 1980s a massive US security effort shut down many Caribbean drug routes, and traffickers were increasingly forced to move their product through Mexico.

Shift in Focus of US Aid to Mexico

While the portion of total US foreign aid to Mexico going to security and counternarcotic efforts is in decline, the portion being used for human rights and institution building is increasing.

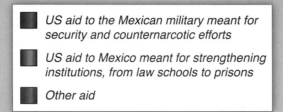

■ US aid to the Mexican military meant for security and counternarcotic efforts

■ US aid to Mexico meant for strengthening institutions, from law schools to prisons

■ Other aid

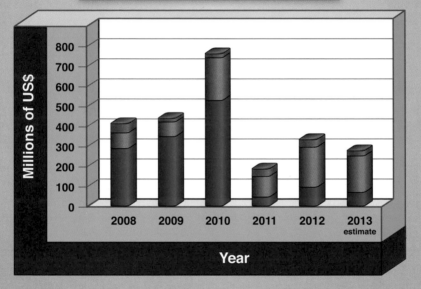

Taken from: Nicholas Casey, "US Shifts Mexico Drug Fight," *Wall Street Journal*, September 17, 2012. http://online.wsj.com.

In 2008, Mexico passed a wide-ranging package of constitutional and legislative reforms that, if and when enacted, will fundamentally transform Mexico's judicial system. The new legal framework introduces oral trials, the presumption of innocence, access to an adequate defense, and strengthens due process. It also establishes alternative arbitration and plea bargaining options to help streamline the legal process, helping prosecutors to prioritize their time and resources more strategically. It bolsters investigation and prosecution tools against organized crime, making it easier to tap phones and to hold suspects, effectively suspending habeas corpus for especially serious crimes. . . .

Focusing on State and Local Efforts

Second, U.S. security support should continue to move beyond the federal level, focusing U.S. resources and programs in Mexico on state and local efforts, as this is where violence and insecurity are most concentrated and devastating. A shift to the local level would also enable policymakers and U.S.-supported programs to recognize and address the varying nature of the violence. In cities such as Ciudad Juárez, local gangs today are perhaps as threatening as transnational drug cartels.

This more local focus will involve expanding the training and professionalization courses available to state and local law enforcement. It should move beyond classes to greater support for the development of systems of standards, police procedures, and evaluation mechanisms for Mexico's local law enforcement, as most of Mexico's police forces lack elements as basic as manuals that lay out standard practices. Drawing on known national and international accrediting agencies and programs such as the Commission on Accreditation for Law Enforcement Agencies (CALEA), the International Association of Directors of Law Enforcement Standards and Training, and the Commission on Peace Officer Standards and Training, the United States can be useful in helping Mexico define and set these guidelines, to which officers can then be held accountable.

In addition, these joint U.S. and Mexican local efforts should concentrate on realizing the so-far-neglected fourth pillar of the Merida Initiative, which calls for building resilient communities. Mexico has seen many instances of innovation in places hit hard by violence, including the business community's involvement in creating a new state police force in Monterrey. . . .

Finally, the United States should prioritize the modernization of the U.S.-Mexico border. This means expanding its roads, bridges, and FAST lanes (express lanes for trusted drivers), as well as increasing the number of U.S. customs officers, agricultural specialists, and support staff that man the ports of entry. The estimated cost of these necessary investments would also be relatively small, with the U.S. Customs and Border Patrol estimating the need for some $6 billion over the next decade. These investments are vital for security, helping to keep out illicit goods and people. Upgrading the border has an added benefit, as it will facilitate legal trade, where consultants estimate losses in the tens of billions of dollars and hundreds of thousands of jobs, due to long border wait times and distances between ports of entry.

The outlined initiatives—many already part of the Merida framework—have a greater chance of reducing violence in Mexico, as they will help strengthen police forces, court systems, and local communities. The border improvements, moreover, will benefit both the U.S. and Mexican economies, which can have indirect positive effects by providing greater legal opportunities to young people. In the end, Mexico's security will depend on the actions and decisions of Mexico. But there is much the United States can do to help or hinder the process. A transition to a justice and a more local level and community-based approach to U.S. security assistance will help Mexico establish more effective and long-lasting tools for combating crime and violence.

Note

1. The Merida Initiative is a partnership launched in 2007 among the United States, Mexico, the nations of Central America, the Dominican Republic, and Haiti to fight organized crime.

EVALUATING THE AUTHOR'S ARGUMENTS

In this viewpoint, Shannon K. O'Neil claims that the United States should help Mexico lower its crime rate to benefit both countries. Why might someone argue that it is not the responsibility of the United States to provide financial support for Mexico's security efforts?

Editor's note: These facts can be used in reports to add credibility when making important points or claims.

Government Reforms in Mexico

According to Americas Market Intelligence:

- President Enrique Peña Nieto's first step toward legislative reform was negotiating the Pact for Mexico with the two main opposition parties: the National Action Party and the Party of the Democratic Revolution. The pact aims to create a joint policy agenda to reform areas such as education, economic deregulation, and energy modernization.

According to Council of the Americas:

- On December 12, 2013, Mexico's Congress passed landmark energy reform that ended a seventy-five-year state monopoly on petroleum and opened the oil and gas industries to private investment.
- Fiscal reforms went into effect in January 2014. Among the reforms was a tax on junk food and sugary drinks and an increase in the income tax rate on upper-income brackets.
- Mexico's political reform was passed by its Congress on December 13, 2013. It established reelection limitations for federal and local congresspersons, senators, and mayors. Senators are now eligible for one reelection, and federal deputies can be reelected up to three times. In addition, the reform stipulates that at least 50 percent of congressional candidacies must be reserved for women.
- Educational reform, passed in December 2012, aimed to create an independent government agency that oversees a teacher-evaluation system. The reform also sought to increase the number of students who complete middle school to 80 percent and those who complete high school to 40 percent.

Mexico's Economy

According to the website Trading Economics:

- The United States is Mexico's main trading partner. The United States accounts for 78 percent of Mexico's total exports and 51 percent of its imports.

According to the Mexican Tourism Board:

- More than 8 percent of Mexico's gross domestic product (GDP) comes from tourism.
- Mexico is ranked tenth in the world for visits by foreign tourists and seventeenth in earnings from tourism.

According to Revenue Watch Institute:

- Oil production is one of the top industries in Mexico.
- In 2011, 33 percent of government income and 20 percent of exports were generated by petroleum.

According to BBC News:

- Cartels in Mexico control the trafficking of drugs from South America to the United States, a trade that brings in an estimated $13 billion a year.

According to the new agency Reuters:

- Six in ten Mexican workers (30 million people) take part in the nations' underground economy.
- The high number of Mexicans working in the underground economy creates a low tax base and has hindered plans to set up a universal social security system.

Mexico and Immigration

According to the Pew Research Center's Hispanic Trends Project:

- Of all current US immigrants, 30 percent were born in Mexico.
- Most of the US unauthorized population comes from Mexico—58 percent in 2012.

- Of all Mexican immigrants in the United States, 51 percent are undocumented.
- In 2011, 6.1 million undocumented Mexican immigrants were living in the United States, down from nearly 7 million in 2007.
- After four decades of a rise in immigration levels from the 1970s through the 2000s, the migration flow from Mexico to the United States experienced a sharp decline during the 2007–2009 US recession and came to a standstill.
- The standstill in migration from Mexico to the United States resulted from many factors, including the weakened US economy, a rise in deportations, a decline in Mexico's birth rates, and improving economic conditions in Mexico.

Mexico's Drug War

According to the Council on Foreign Relations:

- The drug trade makes up 3 to 4 percent of Mexico's $1.2 trillion annual GDP—totaling as much as $30 billion; the underground industry employs at least a half-million people.
- As of March 2014, more than 90 percent of the cocaine in the United States had come through Mexico.

According to CNN:

- Along the US-Mexico border, there are approximately 6,700 licensed firearms dealers in the United States. There is only one legal firearms dealer in Mexico.
- Nearly 70 percent of guns recovered from Mexican criminal activity from 2007 to 2011 had originated from sales in the United States.
- US drug sales garner Mexican drug cartels between $19 billion and $29 billion a year.

According to the *New York Times*:

- In January 2012, the Mexican government reported that 47,515 people had been killed in drug-related violence since late 2006.

Organizations to Contact

The editors have compiled the following list of organizations concerned with the issues debated in this book. The descriptions are derived from materials provided by the organizations. All have publications or information available for interested readers. The list was compiled on the date of publication of the present volume; the information provided here may change. Be aware that many organizations take several weeks or longer to respond to inquiries, so allow as much time as possible for the receipt of requested materials.

Americas Program of the Center for International Policy
Cerrada de Xolalpa 7ª-3
Colonia Tortuga, Mexico
+52 555 324-1201
e-mail: info@cipamericas.org
website: www.cipamericas.org

For more than thirty years, the Americas Program of the Center for International Policy has been a source of news and analysis about movements for social justice within Latin America. The vision of the Americas Program is a "hemisphere where all people—men, women and children—live in peace and have the basic means for a life with dignity and full enjoyment of human rights." The program evaluates the impact of US policies on Latin America, promotes policies that encourage mutual respect and demilitarization in the hemisphere, and strengthens ties among US and Latin American social justice organizations. Based in Mexico City, Mexico, the program uses publications, public speaking, media interviews, and multimedia production to create a dialogue throughout Latin America and strengthen the efforts of social justice movements throughout the hemisphere.

Amnesty International
1 Easton Street
London WC1X 0DW
United Kingdom

+44 207 413 5500; fax: +44 207 956 1157
website: www.amnesty.org

Amnesty International is an organization that fights against abuses of human rights across the globe. The organization was founded in 1961 and now has members in more than 150 countries. The aim of Amnesty International is for "every person to enjoy all the rights enshrined in the Universal Declaration of Human Rights and other international human rights standards." The organization has a network of regional hubs that use research and campaigns as a force for freedom and justice. Amnesty International has a regional section on its website devoted to Mexico that includes news articles as well as an annual report.

Center for US-Mexican Studies, University of California–San Diego
9500 Gilman Drive, #0519
La Jolla, CA 92093-0519
(858) 534-0194
e-mail: usmex@ucsd.edu
website: http://usmex.ucsd.edu

The Center for US-Mexican Studies is a policy research institute at the University of California–San Diego's School of International Relations and Pacific Studies. It has been a source for academic research on Mexico and US-Mexican relations since 1979. Research from the institute has informed the creation, implementation, and evaluation of public policy. The research institute hosts conferences, workshops, and cultural events to promote discourse among government, business, and civic leaders about current issues in Mexico.

Council on Foreign Relations (CFR)
58 E. 68th Street
New York, NY 10065
(212) 434-9400 • fax: (212) 434-9800
website: www.cfr.org

Founded in 1921, the Council on Foreign Relations is an independent, nonpartisan membership organization, think tank, and publisher that focuses on foreign policy issues impacting the United States and other countries. CFR's think tank, the David Rockefeller Studies Program, is made up of fellows who cover major issues shaping the current international agenda. In addition to its think tank, the organization publishes reports, analysis briefs, and the bimonthly magazine *Foreign Affairs*. The Mexico section of CFR's website features interviews, blogs, and numerous multimedia resources about foreign policy issues impacting that country.

Council on Hemispheric Affairs (COHA)
1250 Connecticut Ave., NW, Suite 1-C
Washington, DC 20036
(202) 223-4975 • fax: (202) 223-4979
e-mail: coha@coha.org
website: www.coha.org

Founded in 1975, the Council on Hemispheric Affairs is a nonprofit research organization that promotes the common interests of the Western Hemisphere and raises the visibility of regional affairs. COHA supports open and democratic political processes and does not maintain partisan allegiances. It has consistently condemned authoritarian regimes throughout the hemisphere that fail to provide their populations with political freedoms or economic and social justice. COHA has a section devoted to Mexico on its website that offers news articles and analysis about issues impacting that country.

Justice in Mexico Project (JMP)
University of San Diego
5998 Alcalá Park
San Diego, CA 92110
(619) 260-2299
website: http://justiceinmexico.org

The Justice in Mexico Project is a research initiative based at the University of San Diego that promotes analysis, dialogue, and policy solutions to address a variety of issues impacting Mexico and the US-Mexican border region. The project focuses on three main research areas: security and violence, transparency and accountability, and justice and human rights. Its website offers news articles, reports, working papers, fact sheets, and a blog. The JMP aims to report on issues impacting Mexico, especially at the local level, that are often not covered by mainstream US or international news agencies.

Latin American Network Information Center (LANIC)
Teresa Lozano Long Institute of Latin American Studies
1 University Station D0800
University of Texas
Austin, TX 78712
website: www.lanic.utexas.edu

The Latin American Network Information Center was established at the University of Texas at Austin in 1992. LANIC's mission is to facilitate access to information concerning Latin America for research and academic endeavors. The center's website has become a gateway to Latin America for educators and students as well as private and public sector professionals. LANIC's directories contain one of the largest guides for Latin American content on the Internet. The center's website has a section devoted to Mexico that includes resources on topics such as anthropology, arts and humanities, economy, energy, and government.

Mexican Embassy in the United States
1911 Pennsylvania Ave., NW
Washington, DC 20006
(202) 728-1600
e-mail: mexembusa@sre.gob.mx
website: http://embamex.sre.gob.mx

The Mexican embassy in Washington, DC, is the Mexican diplomatic mission to the United States. The embassy operates consulates general throughout the country. The embassy's website offers the locations of its consulates general as well as articles, fact sheets, and social media links. In 1990, the embassy established the Mexican Cultural Institute of Washington, DC. The goal of the institute is to enrich the relationship between Mexico and the United States by sharing Mexico's vibrant culture with the local community. The institute presents ongoing cultural programs and has become a thriving artistic center.

México: Presidencia de la República
website: http://en.presidencia.gob.mx

The English language version of the current administration's official website features an overview of the Mexican governmental structure, proposed initiatives, and programs. The administration also offers a schedule of upcoming events, press releases, and transcripts from the president's speeches. There are numerous social media links on the website, as well as a blog written by the president and his staff.

Migration Policy Institute (MPI)
1400 Sixteenth Street, NW, Suite 300
Washington, DC 20036
(202) 266-1940
e-mail: info@migrationpolicy.org
website: www.migrationpolicy.org

The Migration Policy Institute is an independent, nonprofit think tank in Washington, DC, dedicated to analyzing the movement of people worldwide. MPI evaluates migration and refugee policies at local, national, and international levels. The institute publishes the online journal *Migration Information Source*, which provides global analysis of international migration and refugee trends. MPI's website features numerous resources on immigration issues impacting Mexico, from journal articles to fact sheets, policy briefs, and books.

North American Congress on Latin America (NACLA)
53 Washington Square South, Floor 4W
New York, NY 10012
(212) 998-8638; fax: (212) 995-4163
website: http://nacla.org

Founded in 1966, NACLA is an independent nonprofit organization that seeks a world in which Latin America and the Caribbean are free from oppression and injustice. The mission of NACLA is to provide information and analysis on the region and on its relationship with the United States for journalists, policy makers, activists, students, and scholars. The organization publishes the quarterly magazine *NACLA Report on the Americas,* hosts an Internet resource center with news and information from Latin America, publishes books and anthologies, administers the Media Accuracy on Latin America initiative, oversees a grant program for young investigative journalists, and produces radio content on Latin American affairs and US policy.

Washington Office on Latin America (WOLA)
1666 Connecticut Ave., NW, Suite 400

Washington, DC 20009
(202) 797-2171
website: www.wola.org

Founded in 1974, the Washington Office on Latin America is a non-governmental organization that promotes human rights, democracy, and social justice. The organization works with partners in Latin America and the Caribbean to shape policies in the United States and abroad. The mission of WOLA is to create a future in which human rights and social justice are the foundation for public policy in Latin America and the Caribbean. WOLA has numerous online resources, from background briefings, publications, and memos. The section of WOLA's website devoted to Mexico includes news articles, analysis and commentary, podcasts, and videos.

Wilson Center Mexico Institute

Ronald Reagan Building and International Trade Center
One Woodrow Wilson Plaza
1300 Pennsylvania Ave., NW
Washington, DC 20004-3027
(202) 691-4000
website: www.wilsoncenter.org

The Wilson Center's Mexico Institute is a research initiative that seeks to improve understanding, communication, and cooperation between Mexico and the United States by encouraging public discussion and proposing policy options. It is overseen by a binational advisory board. The institute focuses on five key issues in US-Mexican relations: security cooperation, economics and competitiveness, migration, border issues, and energy. Its website features news articles, reports, commentary and analysis, and videos.

For Further Reading

Books

Brian Baumgart, *Teens in Mexico*. North Mankato, MN: Capstone, 2007. This book is part of a series that explores the lives of teens around the world. In this title the author examines the heritage and tradition of young people in Mexico.

Anita Brenner and George R. Leighton. *The Wind That Swept Mexico*. Austin: University of Texas Press, 1971. This book offers an introduction to the Mexican Revolution of 1910–1942. The text follows the many different phases of the war and offers a collection of rare photographs.

Jurgen Buchenau, *Mexican Mosaic: A Brief History of Mexico*. Hoboken, NJ: Wiley-Blackwell, 2012. Part of a global history series, this book summarizes Mexico's history since its independence from Spain in 1821 and focuses on the geographical, ethnic, and social diversity within the nation.

Roderic Ai Camp, *Mexico: What Everyone Needs to Know*. New York: Oxford University Press, 2011. Part of the Oxford series What Everyone Needs to Know, this book offers a thorough introduction to Mexico for anyone interested in the nation's past, present, and future.

Ernesto Chavez, *The US War with Mexico: A Brief History with Documents*. Boston: Bedford/St. Martin's, 2007. In this book a history professor examines the US war with Mexico and also provides a collection of historical documents.

Alfredo Corchado, *Midnight in Mexico: A Reporter's Journey Through a Country's Descent into Darkness*. New York: Penguin, 2013. A Mexican American journalist tells of his quest to report on the truth of his country and of his search for home as he covers the Mexican drug war.

David Danelo, *The Border: Exploring the US-Mexican Divide*. Mechanicsburg, PA: Stackpole, 2008. This book offers an investigative report on the physical, political, economic, social, and cultural realities of the US-Mexico border. The author traveled along the border and details the experience of those who live and work there, from businessmen to smugglers, humanitarians, migrants, and border patrol agents.

Alexander S. Dawson, *First World Dreams: Mexico Since 1989.* New York: Zed Books, 2006. A professor of Latin American studies offers a look at Mexico's history since 1989. The author focuses on the nation's growth and reforms as well as issues plaguing the nation, such as income inequality, crime, and human rights abuses.

Ioan Grillo, *El Narco: Inside Mexico's Criminal Insurgency.* London: Bloomsbury, 2011. A journalist takes an investigative look at drug cartels in Mexico and their impact on Mexican society.

Judith Adler Hellman, *The World of Mexican Migrants: The Rock and the Hard Place.* New York: New Press, 2008. The author uses five years of interviews to offer an in-depth look at the lives of Mexican immigrants in the United States.

Z. Anthony Kruszewski, Tony Payan, and Kathleen Staudt, eds. *A War That Can't Be Won: Binational Perspectives on the War on Drugs.* Tucson: University of Arizona Press, 2013. This book includes perspectives on the Mexican drug war from scholars on both sides of the US-Mexico border and proposes solutions for solving the crisis.

Colin M. MacLachlan, *Mexico's Crucial Century, 1810–1910: An Introduction.* Lincoln: University of Nebraska Press, 2010. A history professor provides an accessible guide to the history of Mexico during the century between the nation's independence and the Mexican Revolution.

Shannon K. O'Neil, *Two Nations Indivisible: Mexico, the United States, and the Road Ahead.* New York: Oxford University Press, 2014. In this book, a researcher examines the relationship between Mexico and the United States and contends that the future of the two nations depends on their developing a true partnership.

Chloe Sayer, *Fiesta: Days of the Dead and Other Mexican Festivals.* Austin: University of Texas Press, 2010. Using her travel experiences and the collections of the British Museum, the author details the vast range of annual festivals in Mexico and offers vivid full-color images.

Jo Tuckman, *Mexico: Democracy Interrupted*. New Haven, CT: Yale University Press, 2012. A journalist examines Mexico's history from 2000 to 2012 and reports on the government's accomplishments and shortfalls, as well as the complex challenges that nation faces.

Periodicals and Internet Sources

Dudley Althaus, "Mexico's Energy Reform: 3 Questions with *GlobalPost*'s Dudley Althaus," *GlobalPost*, December 18, 2013. www.globalpost.com.

Peter Andrews, "Mexican Immigration and a Failed State," Center for Immigration Studies, February 2014. http://cis.org.

Homero Aridjis, "The Sun, the Moon and Walmart," *New York Times*, May 1, 2012.

Michael Crowley, "The Committee to Save Mexico," *Time*, February 13, 2014.

Dwight Dyer, Michael Moran, and Gavin Strong. "Mexico's Energy Revolution: A Tank Half-Full," *Forbes*, April 8, 2013.

William Finnegan, "The Kingpins: The Fight for Guadalajara," *New Yorker*, July 2, 2012.

Barbara Frey, "Doing Orwell Proud: 'Human Rights' Slogans in Mexico," Open Democracy, February 3, 2014. www.opendemocracy.net.

Human Rights Watch, "World Report 2014: Mexico." www.hrw.org.

Tim Johnson, "Entrenched Interests Enslave Mexico in a Culture of Hopelessness," *McClatchyDC*, June 17, 2012. www.mcclatchydc.com.

Olga Khazan, "Mexico Is Getting Better, and Fewer Mexicans Want to Leave," *The Atlantic*, April 17, 2013.

Brianna Lee, "Mexico's Drug War," Council on Foreign Relations, March 5, 2014. www.cfr.org.

Gilberto Lopez y Rivas, "Mexico: The Collapse of the Peña Nieto Myth," *Mexico Voices* (blog), November 6, 2013, Carolyn Smith, trans. http://mexicovoices.blogspot.com.

Andres Martinez, "Mexico's Moment," *Weekly Wonk*, December 12, 2013. http://weeklywonk.newamerica.net.

Shannon K. O'Neil, "Viewpoint: Five Myths About Mexico," BBC News, May 1, 2013. www.bbc.com/news.

Ronn Pineo, "Violence in Mexico and Latin America," Council on Hemispheric Affairs, February 21, 2014. www.coha.org.

Sierra Rayne, "Time to Get Tough with Mexico," *Canada Free Press*, July 29, 2013. http://canadafreepress.com.

Javier Sicilia, "A Father's Plea: End the War on Drugs," CNN, September 10, 2012. www.cnn.com.

Peter Watt, "Self-Defense Groups, Sovereignty, and Cross-Border Collaboration with Mexico," *Mexico, Bewildered and Contested* (blog), March 10, 2014. https://nacla.org.

Duncan Wood, "A Look at Mexico's Political Reform: The Expert Take," Wilson Center Mexico Institute, October 16, 2013. http://wilsoncenter.org.

Shannon Young, "American Media Misses the Story on Mexico's Oil Reform," *Texas Observer*, February 10, 2014.

Websites

Center for US-Mexican Studies, University of California, San Diego (http://usmex.ucsd.edu). The institute's website features working papers, publications, articles, photo galleries, and video on everything Mexican.

The History Channel: Mexico (www.history.com/topics/mexico). The Mexico portal page of the History Channel's website provides access to multimedia content on each of the country's thirty-one states and federal district. It also includes educational videos on the country's ancient and modern history.

Mexico: The Presidency (http://en.presidencia.gob.mx). This is the official website of the office of the president in Mexico. The site features transcripts of presidential speeches, a blog, and a multimedia gallery.

Mexico Voices: Addressing Mexico's Challenges (http://mexicovoices.blogspot.com). This blog provides English translations of current news stories from Mexican newspapers and magazines. Using a group of volunteer translators, the blog gives non-Spanish-speaking readers access to important current events and issues in Mexico in near real time.

National Geographic: Mexico (http://travel.nationalgeographic .com/travel/countries/mexico-guide). The Mexico portal of the National Geographic Society's website provides access to the organization's wealth of multimedia content on that country. Sections include travel guides, country facts, and maps, as well as their signature photos and video essays.

North American Congress on Latin America (NACLA): *Mexico, Bewildered and Contested* (https://nacla.org/blog/mexico-bewil dered-contested). This NACLA blog covers Mexican politics and economy and US-Mexican relations, with a particular emphasis on Mexico's complex challenges related to crime, government, and basic survival.

Pew Research Center Hispanic Trends Project (www.pewhispanic .org). This project of a nonpartisan research institution conducts public opinion surveys that aim to illuminate Latino views on a range of social matters and public policy issues. Topics covered include economics and personal finance, Hispanic/Latino identity, education, health care, immigration trends, the Latino vote, technology adoption, and employment. Its website provides access to the annual National Survey of Latinos as well as demographic studies.

Transparency International: Mexico (www.transparency.org /country#MEX). Transparency International is a global coalition of organizations dedicated to fighting corruption. The coalition's website examines corruption worldwide and its section on Mexico features data and research as well as public opinion on corruption issues facing that nation.

Wilson Center Mexico Institute (www.wilsoncenter.org/program /mexico-institute). The Mexico Institute is focused on improving cooperation between Mexico and the United States. The institute promotes research and its website offers commentary, news articles, publications, and multimedia resources.

Index

Picture Credits